Evolution of Morality and Psychopathology of Evil

Also By Craig R. Vander Maas

Evolution of the Bible

Evolution and Syncretism of Religion

Evolution of Morality and Psychopathology of Evil

An Integral and Evolutionary World View
Volume 3

Craig R. Vander Maas

Integral Growth Publishing
Grand Rapids, MI

Integral Growth Publishing
Grand Rapids, MI
www.integralgrowthpublishing.com

Copyright © 2019 by Craig R. Vander Maas.

For information regarding bulk purchases of 10 or more copies, please email: info@integralgrowthpublishing.com

For more information about the author please visit:
www.craigvandermaas.com

Unless otherwise noted, Scripture quotations are from the New Revised Standard Version Bible, copyright © 1989, by the Division of Christian Education of the National Council of the Churches of Christ in the United States of America.

Scripture quotations marked KJV are from the King James Version.

First Edition
ISBN 9780997238822 pbk

Blessed are the poor in spirit, for theirs is the kingdom of heaven.

Blessed are those who mourn, for they will be comforted.

Blessed are the meek, for they will inherit the earth.

Blessed are those who hunger and thirst for righteousness, for they will be filled.

Blessed are the merciful, for they will receive mercy.

Blessed are the pure in heart, for they will see God.

Blessed are the peacemakers, for they will be called children of God.

Blessed are those who are persecuted for righteousness' sake, for theirs is the kingdom of heaven.

Jesus (Matthew 5)

Christianity

In everything do to others as you would have them do to you; for this is the law and the prophets.

Jesus (Matthew 7:12)

Do to others as you would have them do to you.

Jesus (Luke 6:31)

For the whole law is summed up in a single commandment, "You shall love your neighbor as yourself."

St. Paul (Galatians 5:14)

Judaism

You shall not take vengeance or bear a grudge against any of your people, but you shall love your neighbor as yourself: I am the Lord.

Leviticus 19:18

What is hateful to you, do not do to your fellow; this is the whole Torah; the rest is the explanation; go and learn.

Hillel the Elder

Buddhism

Hurt not others in ways that you yourself would find hurtful.

Udanavarga 5:18

Hinduism

One should never do that to another which one regards as injurious to one's own self. This in brief, is the rule of dharma. Other behavior is due to selfish desires.

Brihaspati, Mahabharata
(Anusasana Parva, Setion CXIII, Verse 8)

Jainism

Killing a living being is killing one's own self; showing compassion to a living being is showing compassion to oneself. He who desires his own good, should avoid causing any harm to a living being.

Suman Suttam, verse 151

Confucianism

Never impose on others what you would not choose for yourself.

Confucius, Analects XV.24

Mencius

Try your best to treat others as you would wish to be treated yourself and you will find that this is the shortest way to benevolence.

Mencius VII.A.4

Islam

Love for your brother what you love for yourself.

Muhammad, Hadith 13

Contents

Introduction

In my first book "Evolution of the Bible" my goal was to demonstrate how Judaism and Christianity evolved over time, and that in understanding the Bible one needed to keep in mind the time periods in which the various writings were composed. One shouldn't conceive of the Bible as being a single composition; it was written by numerous individuals over a 1,500 year period. All of these writers, in sharing their thoughts about God, had their own personal beliefs and biases and cultural influences. Both Judaism and Christianity evolved and changed as religions through the centuries. The Bible came together centuries later and was the result of decisions by groups of people who decided from among many scriptures what writings they believed should be in a canon. Many people believe we know the mind of God because it's in the Bible; actually what's in the Bible reflects the beliefs of people who think the chosen writings reflect the mind of God. In the early creeds of the church there is no mention of a Bible or a canon of literature. It did not achieve its exalted position really until the Reformation when Martin Luther opined *sola scriptura* (the belief that the scriptures alone are the infallible words of God).

In my second book "Evolution and Syncretism of Religion" my goal was to demonstrate that all religions evolved, and that the various religions influenced each other. The word "syncretism" in regards to religion refers to the blending and amalgamation of beliefs, rituals and cultures. In contrast to the widespread belief of Christians that in the beginning there was the *true* religion that later heresies corrupted, that in fact, all religions including Judaism and Christianity developed and evolved. Although not stated explicitly in this second book, I am really arguing against the belief in "special revelation", i.e. that God literally spoke to a few individuals in ages long past, and that the Bible is the literal words of God. I argue against special revelation, magic and supernaturalism. When I grew up I was taught and I believed that religion was the result of revelation; I now believe religion is the result of evolution.

I recently examined a new book which presents a critique of progressive Christianity and arguments for Biblical literalism and proto-orthodox positions. I was encouraged to read ,"We should not believe in anything, religious or other-wise, unless the evidence supports it." (Jensen, 2017) Yay! So far so good! I was later disappointed to read from this author that we should accept the Bible as special revelation because it is self-evident. Based on its "splendor, glory, beauty, and power...it testifies of itself that it is special reve-lation....It is clear to anyone who approaches it with an open mind that it gives to us the fullness of special revelation. We are in need of no more, period." Of course this rationale is not "evidence". It was evident to people centuries ago that the world was flat, but of course that was not true.

If the Bible is the literal, inerrant and direct word of God, I would not expect contradictions. For example, why are there

2

two separate and contradictory creation stories in Genesis? Why in the book of Genesis is it reported that Noah's ark was filled with a pair of every species, while elsewhere in Genesis it is reported that seven pairs of each species was put into the ark? These types of contradictions abound.

If in the Ten Commandments God forbids killing, why did he direct Joshua to commit genocide: "they devoted to destruction by the edge of the sword all in the city, both men and women, young and old, oxen, sheep, and donkeys." (Joshua 6:21). Also in the Ten Commandments God forbids adultery, but yet his Godly followers Abraham and Isaac out of fear are willing to lie about the identity of their wives and are willing give them to King Abimelech to have sexually. Abraham and Isaac are never chastised by God for this. Lot's wife is turned into a pillar of salt for looking back at the destruction of Sodom and Gomorrah, but just a few verses later in the 19th chapter of Genesis there is no mention of chastisement or punishment for Lot being drunk and having consensual sex with his two daughters.

If the criteria for being "special revelation" is "splendor, glory, beauty, and power", I think a better case for special revelation is made for Beethoven's Ninth Symphony or Raphael's painting "Transfiguration" than the Bible.

I grew up being taught and believing that the Bible was the inerrant, literal word of God, and no evidence was presented to me to support this. I was taught nothing about the history of the Bible. We believed this out of tradition. We believed this because the church taught us this. We believed it because of "faith". Or we believed it because we liked believing it.

I have read many attacks on science by fundamentalists and evangelicals because of the belief that scientific teachings were in contradiction to the teachings of the Bible. They disputed biology, astronomy, geology and other scientific disciplines because they perceived that it contradicted God, and how could God be wrong? I heard fantastical rationales to argue against scientific findings; for example, in order to argue a young earth (6,000 year) world view, I've heard it hypothesized that God planted bones millions of years old (I guess just to confuse us). While fundamentalists went to great lengths to try to provide some type of explanation for scientific findings that went against their beliefs, I have yet to hear any actual evidence for the Bible being the literal, inerrant words of God.

While my views have changed based on the evidence, I still believe in God, and I am still a Christian- I follow and venerate the teachings of Jesus. World views and beliefs need to evolve, and our beliefs should be based on evidence, truth. Even the prominent early church father, Augustine (in "The Literal Meaning of Genesis"), warned Christians about appearing foolish for explaining the natural world using scripture. Words of the apostle Paul are also relevant here:

"When I was a child, I spoke like a child, I thought like a child, I reasoned like a child; when I became an adult, I put an end to childish ways." (First Corinthians 13:11).

Our "faith", beliefs, and understandings should evolve beyond the simple conceptions and world view of a third grader. Throughout my life I have sought to understand God and the universe based on *evidence*. The reason I began this book series with a book on the history of the Bible was because of the common response given to me by fundamentalists and evangelicals to this evidence, i.e. that there was

4

the conflicting "evidence" that they perceived in the Bible, and that anything found in the Bible would trump anything else. Yet I also found that these individuals had little knowledge about where the Bible actually came from. Mostly they believed it literally because somebody told them to believe it.

This brings us to the third book of this series; the subject of morality and "good" and "evil". I, like most evangelicals, grew up believing that good was what God said was good, and evil was what God said was evil. I believed morality was *revealed*. I believed it was the result of God's revelation. It didn't matter why God made these determinations; simply, God said it and I needed to follow it. Pertinent is the quotation from Isaiah 55:8-9 that I cited in my first book:

For my thoughts are not your thoughts, nor are your ways my ways, says the Lord. For as the heavens are higher than the earth, so are my ways higher than your ways and my thoughts than your thoughts.

Also pertinent is the bumper sticker I once saw:

God said it. I believe it. That settles it.

I now believe that morality is the result of evolution, not revelation. This book, particularly chapter one entitled "History of Morality", is an explanation for this belief. One of the earliest stories about good and evil to have been written in the Hebrew scriptures would have been the story of Adam and Eve in the Garden of Eden. In this story about the first man and woman, God has but one rule: do not eat of the tree of knowledge of good and evil. Of course, despite this being an easy law to avoid, our protagonists break the rule and are thereby cursed. In fact, some believe that not only were Adam and Eve cursed, but all of humanity was cursed. This is known as *original sin*; because of Adam and Eve's disobedience, all of humankind is now in a state of sinfulness or evil.

Taking this story literally really makes no sense to me. Why would God not want humankind to know the difference between good and evil? Some see this myth as the story about humankind's loss of innocence- a story of the evolution from being animals to being sentient, rational beings. It is a step toward becoming a *God*. The story of the Garden of Eden tells about another special tree planted by God: the tree of life. Many believe this tree represents immortality- yet another step toward becoming a God.

What is morality?

Morality can be defined as upright conduct, or principles concerning the distinction between what is right or wrong, good or evil. The term "ethics" is often used as a synonym, although "ethics" can also refer to the standards of behavior particular to a profession. For example, in my profession as a psychologist it would be unethical for me to date somebody I was doing psychotherapy with, although the behavior is not necessarily immoral.

All of the major religions consider the "golden rule" to be an important concept in regards to morality. The various iterations of this moral precept are listed in the beginning of this book. Constructs that are important to the Golden Rule are empathy, sympathy, and altruism. Empathy can be defined as the capacity to understand the point of view of another person so that one vicariously shares the other person's feelings, perceptions, and thoughts. Sympathy can be defined as an expression of understanding and care for someone else's suffering. Altruism can be defined as putting others' interests before one's own sometimes to the point of sacrificing one's own interests or life in the process.

Philosophy

The discipline of philosophy deals with the topic of morality quite extensively. There are five major branches of philosophy: aesthetics (the study of beauty), logic (the study of argument and the principles of reasoning), epistemology (the study of knowledge), metaphysics (the study of the nature of reality), and ethics (the study of morality). This last branch obviously is very germane to this book, and shortly I will summarize some of the controversies in the field. Epistemology and metaphysics are also germane to this book, and all five branches are relevant to the entire book series.

One of the philosophical disputes in the field is the question of where morality comes from. Many people would assert that morality comes from God. As I previously mentioned, this was the conception that I grew up with. Things were right or wrong because God said so. Period. What then is the cause of evil? This question has been debated much by theologians. Are "sin" and evil the same things? Or are they qualitatively different rather than quantitatively different. If God is omnipotent (all-powerful) and all-loving, why does God allow evil to exist? Is it that God really does not have the power to banish evil, or does God just not really care? In other words is God unwilling or unable? Or is there another explanation?

When talking about the concept of evil, a distinction is often made between "moral evil" and "natural evil". The former refers the evil committed by humans, e.g. killing, stealing, bullying, lying, etc. "Natural evils" would include earthquakes, hurricanes, tsunamis, etc. If humans do not cause these natural evils, who does? God?

Can there be morality without religion? Certainly we all know of religious people who have committed acts of evil, and non-religious people who appear to be the epitome of good. Can there be morality without God? Can people be moral without the threat of hell or without a promise of a glorious afterlife in heaven? Might people be moral simply out of "enlightened self-interest", i.e. living life knowing that if everyone tried to do good and avoid evil, the world would be a tremendously better place for everyone?

Are there moral absolutes, or is morality relative? People who subscribe to moral relativism suggest that morality is a cultural construct, and that there are no absolute rights and wrongs. Proponents of this view suggest that individuals need to decide for themselves what to do in various situations. Moral decisions are based on feeling and intuition. It is reflected in the 1960s slogan: "If it feels good, do it." People who claim that there are moral absolutes probably most frequently cite God as the reason: this is known as "divine command theory". However, there are others who cite other reasons for believing in moral absolutes. Thomas Aquinas argued that there were *natural laws* which people should subscribe to in addition to believing in a supernatural basis for morality. Immanuel Kant sought to establish moral absolutes based completely on reason. He stressed that we should act out of a "good will" and duty based on reason and principle rather than desire for particular consequences.

This brings up another argument in the field of ethics, i.e. whether behaviors should be considered moral or immoral based on principles or based on the consequences of an action. Kant would advocate for the former. He believed that there are absolutes that should be followed regardless of the consequences. Aquinas would agree; he believed in *natural laws*. Many religions would subscribe to this as well, i.e. that moral absolutes come from God. These *nonconsequentialists* adhere to *deontological* theories of morality. Deontology is the study of the nature of duty and obligation. The other viewpoint is of the *consequentialists* who follow *teleological* theories of morality. Teleology is a philosophy that stresses the importance of the final purpose.

A related question is about whether evil is due to the conse- quences of behaviors or due to the intention. Is what made Hitler evil the number of people who suffered and died at his direction, or was it his "heart", his character that made him evil. If someone has the intention to shoot up a school but is apprehended before it happens, is that person less evil than someone who has successfully completed such an act? Our criminal justice system will give stiffer punishments based on the actual consequences of behaviors. For example, there are stiffer punishments for murder than for attempted mur- der. For those who commit multiple murders, there is increased time in prison for each additional victim, i.e. three counts of murder as opposed to two. But should morality be measured differently? Jesus seemed to think so. He said, "You have heard that it was said 'You shall not murder", and 'whoever murders shall be liable to judgment.' But I say to you that if you are angry with a brother or sister, you will be liable to judgment." He said, "You heard that it was said,'You shall not commit adultery.' But I say to you that everyone who looks at a woman with lust has already committed adultery with her in his heart." For Jesus, character mattered.

The consequentialists can be delineated into three major camps: egoism, altruism and utilitarianism. The egoists believe that everyone should act in his or her own best interest but then also take responsibility for the consequences of their actions. Egoists argue that this system fits best with true capitalism. Others would argue that this really is not a moral system at all, and in fact might reflect a lack of morality. Perhaps the best known proponent of egoism is Ayn Rand. Her thoughts are expounded in her novel *Atlas Shrugged* and in her non-fiction book *The Virtue of Selfishness:*

The basic social principle of the Objectivist ethics is that just as life is an end in itself, so every living human being is an end in himself, not the means to the ends or the welfare of others- and, therefore, that man must live for his own sake, neither sacrificing himself to others nor sacrificing others to himself. To live for his own sake means that the achievement of his own happiness is man's highest moral purpose. (p. 30).

Rand argues against "altruism" in her book *The Virtue of Selfishness*, but what she appears to be arguing against is a philosophy called altruism that advocates that humans should *always* act in the interest of others over and above oneself. This is somewhat different than the definition of altruism that I presented above that states that *sometimes* people put others' interests above their own. An example would be a soldier sacrificing his life for his country or the firemen who gave up their lives in the World Trade Centers to help save the lives of others after 911. Jesus said to "love your neighbor as yourself", not *instead* of yourself or *above* yourself. This philosophy is known as *utilitarianism.*

Two philosophers who were proponents of utilitarianism are Jeremy Bentham and John Stuart Mill. The utilitarians believe that acts that are right or moral are those acts that bring about the greatest good for *all*. Similarly, rules and laws should be established that bring about the greatest good for all. For both egoists and utilitarians, it is the consequences of actions and laws that are most important.

The term *teleological* means to aim at some purpose or ultimate goal or ending. A school of ethics that fits into this category is something called *virtue ethics*. This moral theory stresses the development of virtuous character in human beings and strives for the development of human excellence. Important early proponents of this theory include Aristotle in the West, and Confucius and his disciple Mencius in the East.

Aristotle asserted that the goal for human beings was to reason well in order to have a whole and complete life. He believed that humans have natural ethical tendencies, but that these need to be developed by training and practice. By practice they become a part of our character. Confucius and Mencius agree that virtues are developed through self-cultivation until they become habits, and that it is part of the process of becoming fully human. Both Aristotle and Confucius strove for the development of superior human beings. Many modern proponents of virtue ethics advocate less emphasis on following rules and laws and more emphasis on developing virtuous human beings. Legalism has not worked well for the betterment of the world! Aristotle believed that the universe is moving toward a final ending. Pierre Telhard De Chardin termed this the *omega point*. Friedrich Hegel wrote that history is the unfolding of the *absolute mind* to achieve God's ultimate realization, i.e. a state of perfection. The evolution of morality and spirituality is crucial in this journey to the omega point, I believe, and this will be explored further in this book and throughout this book series.

Another important topic in the philosophical field of ethics is the question of freedom versus determinism. Actually, the issue probably has more to do with the philosophical sub-field of metaphysics than ethics. The question has to do with how much behaviors are caused/determined by things outside of ourselves. In other words, is everything just cause and effect? Is what we do just *effect* from various other events? The most well known proponent of this is the psychologist and behaviorist, B.F. Skinner. He believed that free will was an illusion, and that all human (and other animal) behavior is dependent on the consequences of other behaviors. We think something because of prior stimuli. We feel something because of prior stimuli. We do things because of prior stimuli. We really don't make conscious decisions; our decisions are based completely on prior behaviors. This view is called hard determinism. It maintains that *all* events are caused, and there is no such thing as free will or freedom. Everything is *stimulus-response*.

Underlying this viewpoint would seem to be Newtonian physics and the belief that everything that exists in the universe is physical in nature. There are no allowances made for mental or spiritual processes or for consciousness. Can human beings transcend physical laws, or are we merely physical, responding to physical laws in the same way that atoms, molecules, and rocks do? Even if one believes that there is nothing but the *physical* world, new discoveries in quantum physics would suggest that the universe is not so neat and tidy and predictable as once thought by Newtonian physics. Walter Heisenberg, the German physicist, articulated the "Uncertainty Principle" which suggests that on the subatomic level, the physical universe is very unpredictable.

There was a quite similar belief system in the religion in which I grew up called *predestination,* or the *doctrine of election.* This doctrine was taught by John Calvin. It is described in the Westminster Confession of Faith, which is one of the major documents that describe Reformed theology. It states that God "freely and unchangeably ordained whatsoever comes to pass." In other words, everything that happens in the world is preordained by God. Everything that happens is by plan. This is, by the way, a minority Christian viewpoint.

In contrast to hard determinism is *soft* determinism. This is the belief that there are many outside factors which significantly affect how we think, how we feel, how we act, and who we are. However, it also allows for choices, i.e. free will. Soft determinism suggests that we have some ability to affect our lives and our futures. It suggests we have the ability to make moral choices, which the hard determinists would say is only an illusion. Two important past theorists that I would consider as soft determinists are Karl Marx and Sigmund Freud. Marx wrote that people are determined by economic and social factors. Freud wrote that people are determined by childhood experiences and the unconscious.

I would consider myself a soft determinist. There are many factors that strongly effect who we are. One factor is genetics. I recently had genetic testing done by "23and Me". While the report about my ancestry was uninteresting and no surprise, the report also gave information about genetic risk for various medical conditions as well as likely traits that I have. It also told me that I have a small amount of neanderthal DNA, as do most northern Europeans. In regards to traits, it correctly predicted that I have no back hair, have no bald spots, have no dimples, have no cleft chin, have no early hair loss, have brown eyes, prefer salty to sweet tastes, and have the ability to detect the odor of asparagus in urine (apparently some people can't). In the future genetics testing will be used increasingly in medicine. Already genetic testing is increasingly utilized to determine if individuals are fast or slow metabolizers for various medications.

Traumatic events that happen to us also affect who we are, particularly when they occur very early in childhood. Traumas affect us not only psychologically, but they also change our brains. Specifically, there is evidence of shrinkage of the hippocampus, an important brain structure for memory, that correlates with childhood maltreatment. Trauma has effects on the *HPA Axis* (which stands for hypothalamic-pituitary-adrenal). The end result is an increase in cortisol which damages the hippocampus.

There was an important study completed by Anda *et al* (2006) in which 17,337 adult HMO members were surveyed about 8 adverse childhood traumas: emotional, physical and sexual abuse, household dysfunction, substance abuse, mental illness, mother treated violently, incarcerated household member, and parental separation or divorce. As the number of adverse childhood traumas increased, the number of behavioral problems and psychiatric symptoms increased. This includes promiscuity, anger, partner violence, panic attacks, depression, anxiety, hallucinations, obesity, somatic complaints, smoking, and use of injectable drugs. One cannot assume causation when there are correlations, but the strength of these correlations were remarkable.

Both nature (genetics) and nurture (upbringing) have profound effects on who we are. However, we don't need to be held hostage to either. After all, what would be the purpose of psychotherapy if this were not the case? Insight oriented psychotherapies such as psychoanalysis help us to make conscious unconscious and repressed thoughts and motivations that keep us stuck. Cognitive therapies help us change irrational thoughts and beliefs. When we think differently, we feel differently. Psychotherapy cannot change a fact such as being sexually abused in childhood and perhaps not having protective parents. I can't change history, but I can change present day thoughts and feelings about the past. It really is not the past that is the problem- it is the present day thoughts and feelings. And as to genetics, it is possible to choose to make changes to counteract this as well. If cardiovascular disease runs in my family, I can choose to eat healthily, keep my weight down, exercise regularly, can choose not to smoke, and use medications to keep my blood pressure and cholesterol levels low.

Some of these philosophical issues of morality that I've touched upon in this introduction will be revisited later on in this book. This book is divided into four chapters. In chapter one I will give a history of morality, particularly exploring how the concepts of "heaven" and "hell" and "demons" developed and evolved. In chapter two I will discuss the concept of evil as being psychopathology. Throughout history the opposite concept has predominated, i.e. that various psychopathologies were considered to be the result of evil, e.g. psychosis, seizures, etc. In chapter three I will suggest that "sin" or immorality is the result of humankind's deficits in moral development. In chapter four I will discuss how all of this applies to our lives. How should we live our lives in order to be moral people? What does it mean to live a Godly life? I will suggest that these deficits in morality (and spiritual development) are the major problems facing humankind. I then will include in an appendix a case study; the subject being Donald J. Trump.

Chapter One

History of Morality

So where does morality come from? Many believe that morality predates religion rather than being the result of religion. In researching this my initial thoughts were to investigate early hunter-gatherer societies to find the early beginnings of morality. But did morality actually develop much earlier with species other than homo sapiens? Do other animals today have some sense of morality?

Animals and Morality

In the introduction to this book I defined morality as "upright conduct" or a sense of right from wrong. I stated that constructs such as empathy, sympathy and altruism were important for the development of morality. Several researchers believe that several species of animals do have some sense of morality (and conversely immorality).

Empathy I defined as the capacity to understand the point of view of another person so that one vicariously shares the other person's feelings, perceptions, and thoughts. Bekoff and Pierce (2009) conclude "there's mounting scientific evidence that animals, even rodents, have the capacity to feel empathy." They also conclude that "empathy is an ancient capacity, probably present in all mammals." They report that the evidence for empathy in animals comes from several fields of research, especially ethology, psychology and neuroscience. "There is some highly suggestive narrative and empirical evidence for empathy in elephants, several cetacean species (especially bottlenose dolphins and toothed whales), rats and mice, social carnivores, and primates."

One very interesting area of research into empathy has to do with *mirror neurons*. These were investigated in the 1980s and 1990s by a group of Italian neurophysiologists. They placed electrodes in areas of the premotor cortex of macaque monkeys and were able to study individual neurons. They discovered that these neurons not only fired when the animals did various behaviors (such as reaching for pieces of food) but also when they observed a person doing the same behavior. Some neuroscientists such as Marco Iacoboni of UCLA, Vittorio Gallese of the University of Parma, and Vilayanur Tamachandran of UC San Diego, hypothesize that mirror neurons may be an important neural mechanism underlying the development of empathy, although at present this is an unproven theory. There is also some evidence for mirror neurons in humans, although the evidence is from fMRI scans (functional magnetic resonance imaging) rather than direct evidence from electrodes being placed into people's brains, which of course could not be done with humans.

Another important class of neurons that might be important to the development of empathy are *spindle cells*, also known as von Economo neurons. In addition to being found in the brains of humans, they also are found in chimpanzees, bonobos, orangutans and gorillas as well as species of dolphins, porpoises, and whales and Asian and African elephants. Interestingly these are the most intelligent and socially sensitive species on earth.

Bekoff and Pierce (2009) note "there are many anecdotal accounts from marine biologists of cetaceans displaying empathy." This includes incidences of whales ending up beached due to coming to the aid of another whale in distress. Bekoff and Pierce also note that "elephants have been observed to be extremely empathic". They cite several anecdotal accounts of elephants coming to the aid of sick and disabled comrades and also grieving the deceased. These are accounts of not only empathy but also sympathy.

I defined *sympathy* as an expression of understanding and care for someone else's suffering. The esteemed Dutch primatologist and ethologist Frans De Waal (2013) said, "Empathy can be quite passive, reflecting mere sensitivity, whereas sympathy is outgoing. It expresses concern for others combined with an urge to ameliorate their situation." "Chimpanzees rescue each other from leopard attacks. Squirrels give alarm calls that warn others of danger. Elephants try to lift up fallen comrades." Bekoff and Pierce (2009) also give numerous examples of animals showing empathy and sympathy for members of other species, including dolphins protecting humans from a great white shark.

Altruism is putting others' interests before one's own sometimes to the point of sacrificing one's own interests or life in the process. De Waal (1996) says, "Altruism is not limited to our species. Indeed, its presence in other species, and the theoretical challenge this represents, is what gave rise to sociobiology- the contemporary study of animal (including human) behavior from an evolutionary perspective. Aiding others at a cost or risk to oneself is widespread in the animal world."

Why from an evolutionary standpoint does altruism exist? Wouldn't the principles of natural selection predict that organisms would do everything they could to benefit themselves and their offspring rather than being self-sacrificial and doing something against their own self-interests? Not only would the theory of natural selection appear to suggest motivation for selfishness, Calvinist Protestantism also suggests that mankind is basically evil due to original sin and that by following the laws of God we are going against our nature. English biologist Thomas Henry Huxley (1825-95), an advocate of Charles Darwin's theories, also believed that our nature was to be selfish, and that to be moral we had to fight against our nature. Frans De Waal (2006) labels this view as *veneer theory*, i.e. that morality is a thin veneer hiding an underlying selfish and brutish nature.

Charles Darwin, himself, however, viewed morality in evolutionary terms; his views on this were expressed in *The Descent of Man and Selection in Relation to Sex (*1982). So why would morality evolve? Frans De Waal wrote quite extensively on this topic in his book *Primates and Philosophers* (2006). De Waal mentions several theorists who see morality as being a natural inclination of human beings. These theorists include Aristotle, Thomas Aquinas, David Hume and Edward Westermarck whom De Waal said "deserves a central position in any debate about the origin of morality, since he was the first scholar to promote an integrated view including both humans and animals and both culture and evolution."

Central to an explanation of why morality might evolve is a theory known as *reciprocal altruism*, which was explained by Robert Trivers (1971). Reciprocal altruism is different from *mutualism,* which is the cooperation between humans or other animals to accomplish a goal that mutually benefits both of them. An example would be bands of early hunter-gathers working together to kill a wooly mammoth. They then share the meat of the animal. Reciprocity involves acts that are beneficial to the recipient but costly to the giver. Populations benefit as a result. As De Waal (2006) explains "Evolution favors animals that assist each other if by doing so they achieve long-term benefits of greater value than the benefits derived from going it alone and competing with others."

A criterion for reciprocal altruism reported by Trivers (1971) is that there is a small cost to the giver but great benefit to the taker. An example given by Trivers is birds who give warning calls about predators; while it puts the calling bird at mildly increased danger, it greatly benefits the rest of the population. A human example of reciprocal altruism is of a good swimmer taking personal risk to save a drowning person. Trivers (1971) says "given the universal and nearly daily practice of reciprocal altruism among humans today, it is reasonable to assume that it has been an important factor in recent human evolution and that the underlying emotional dispositions affecting altruistic behavior have important genetic components."

I agree with Trivers, De Waal, and Darwin that morality appears to be the result of evolution, and that species including homo sapiens benefit in the long run as the result. Aren't we better off as a species, for example, when a good swimmer takes some risk to save a drowning person? There are numerous examples of how the human race benefits by individuals taking some risk to help others- even complete strangers. It is my belief that our species benefits from and evolves as the result of altruism and that selfishness is an impediment to evolution. This idea will be further elaborated in this volume.

De Waal (2006) maintains that "Reciprocity is of course also at the heart of the Golden Rule, which remains unsurpassed as a summary of human morality. To know that some of the psychology behind this rule may exist in other species, along with the required empathy, bolsters the idea that morality, rather than being a recent innovation, is part of human nature."

Zahn-Waxler has researched the development of altruism. She said cognitive and psychoanalytic theories suggest altruism does not develop in children until at least five to seven years old. However, her own research suggests children begin to comfort others in distress as early as just past age one. She visited homes in which the family members were instructed to feign sadness (sobbing), pain (crying) or distress (choking). Children responded by patting and hugging victims, rubbing hurts, etc. "Virtually all of the children studied showed this early capacity for concern for the welfare of another being. This uniformity suggests that altruism is a biological given, 'wired' in and ready for expression given sufficient physical, cognitive, and emotional growth." (Zahn-Waxler et al., 1984). An additional unplanned finding to the study was that pets also showed concern over family members' distress. They responded by hovering over the victims or putting their heads in their laps.

Animals that are capable of moral behavior are those that have the capacity for empathy, altruism and complex cooperative behaviors. Bekoff and Parker (2009) said "candidates include bonobos, chimpanzees, elephants, wolves, hyenas, dolphins, whales, and rats." If animals can be moral, they also can be immoral. Empathy allows for the capacity to understand suffering, and this capacity makes cruelty possible. What does it mean for an animal to be immoral? Is it immoral for a lion to kill a zebra?

I recently went on safaris in southern Africa, and our guide told us that we would not want to see an actual kill by a lion or leopard. He said it is not the quick and clean event we might see on television. Rather the kills are very brutal; animals may scream in agony and terror for a half hour before finally dying. Is the lion cruel? Is the lion immoral? I do not believe so; the lion is responding to hunger, not a desire to be cruel. The lion is behaving according to the social norms of lions. De Waal (2013) noted that the eminent ethologist Konrad Lorenz defined aggression as being *within-species* behavior, not the normal behaviors of carnivores to eat. Also it should be noted that not only carnivores are aggressive; I learned on my safaris that the so-called "big five" game animals are so classified because they are the most dangerous animals to hunt on foot. Three of these five are herbivores, i.e. rhinoceros, elephant and cape buffalo.

The Great Apes and Immorality

Our species, Homo sapiens, belong to the scientific class of Mammalia (Mammals). Empathy, a basic building block of morality, is mostly a mammalian trait. Other scientific classes of vertebrates which include birds, amphibians, reptiles and fish do not generally display empathy, sympathy or altruism.

The species closest to our own are the other members of the scientific family of Hominidae, also known as the "Great Apes". The genus within this family that is most genetically distant from us is *Pongo* (the orangutan), followed by *Gorilla*, followed by *Pan* (the chimpanzee and bonobo). Interestingly, chimpanzees and bonobos are closer genetically to humans than they are to gorillas.

- The human lineage diverged from that of the orang-utan about 15 million years ago.

- The human lineage diverged from that of the gorilla about 10 million years ago.

- The human lineage diverged from that of the chimpanzee about 7 million years ago.

As the capabilities to be moral have evolved, so too it would seem has the capability to be immoral. Let's start with the orangutans, our most distant relative of the family of Hominidae. "Among orangutans, rape accounts for one-third to one-half or more of all copulations. Even among chimpanzees, where rape is a good deal rarer, it probably still happens as often as among many human populations." "Rape occurs much more commonly among the great apes than among most animals." (Wrangham and Peterson, 1996)

Infanticide is prominent in gorilla populations. While gorillas are generally relaxed, gentle and affectionate with each other, male gorillas have a habit of killing the infants of other males. "In the sample, 38 percent of infants died before they were three years old, and at least 37 percent of these deaths were judged to be from infanticide, or about one infant in seven, overall. The figures suggest that the average gorilla female experiences infanticide at least once in her lifetime." (Wrangham and Peterson, 1996)

Other than human beings, chimpanzees might be the only other species that kills its own kind deliberately. Other species may get into intense fights, but the goal is to defeat their opponent, not to kill them. "Out of four thousand mammals and ten million or more other animal species" it is only chimpanzees and humans that conduct lethal raids into other communities of their same species. (Wrangham and Peterson, 1996). In other words, only humans and chimpanzees commit murder.

"During these raids on other communities, the attackers act as they do while hunting monkeys, except that the target 'prey' is a member of their own species. And their assaults, as we have seen, are marked by a gratuitous cruelty- tearing off pieces of skin, for example, twisting limbs until they break, or drinking a victim's blood- reminiscent of acts that among humans are regarded as unspeakable crimes during peacetime and atrocities during war." (Wrangham and Peterson, 1996).

Bonobos

A species very similar to the chimpanzee is the bonobo, which is a little smaller and more slender than the chimpanzee. It is believed that their populations diverged about a million years ago, perhaps due to the Congo River which acted as a barrier preventing their populations from interbreeding. All three species (bonobos, chimpanzees and humans) share about the same amount of DNA, i.e. about 98.6 %), but about 1.6% of our DNA is shared with bonobos but not chimps, and about 1.6% of our DNA is shared with chimps and not bonobos. Scientists believe the chimps and bonobos' common ancestor was more like a chimpanzee than a bonobo.

Behaviorally, chimpanzees and bonobos are quite different from each other. Among bonobos there are no reported incidences of rapes of females, battering of females or killing of infants. There also is evidence that the two sexes are equal and co-dominant. Bonobos have none of the violent behaviors of chimpanzees. They seem to subscribe to the old 1960s slogan of "make love not war". And the sex is both hetero and homosexual "It is well known at zoos that chimpanzee strangers need to be kept apart at all cost until they have become acquainted; otherwise one may be facing a bloodbath. The bonobos at the sanctuary, however, produced an orgy instead. They mixed freely, turning potential enemies into friends." "The presence of food normally induces rivalry, but the bonobos engaged in sexual contact, played together, and happily shared the food side by side. The chimpanzees, by contrast, had trouble overcoming their competitiveness. For two species to react so differently to the exact same setup leaves little doubt about a temperamental difference." (De Waal, 2013).

Early Homo sapiens

Behaviorally, early humans were much more like chimpanzees than bonobos. It seems to be a fallacy than hunter-gatherer societies were peaceful and gentle. "Statistics challenge the notion of the gentle forager. A global assessment of the ethnographies for thirty-one hunter-gather societies found that 64 percent of them engaged in warfare once every two years, 26 percent fought wars less often, and only 10 percent were considered to fight wars rarely or never. So the record suggests regular, almost constant war for most foraging cultures." (Wrangham and Peterson, 1996).

However, our ancestors also could be altruistic. De Waal (2013) notes "our ancestors supported individuals who contributed little to society. Survival of the weak, the handicapped, the mentally retarded, and others who posed a burden is seen by paleontologists as a milestone in the evolution of compassion." De Waal suggests that morality predates current civilizations and religions by at least a hundred millennia.

Early Religion

I wrote about the development of religion in my book "Evolution and Syncretism of Religion". Many historians, including the great social anthropologist Sir Edward Burnett Tyler, believed that one of the earliest religious conceptions was of *animism*. This is the belief that everything has a spiritual essence (a soul), even non-living things, but particularly animals and humans. Burials of humans began in the paleolithic period, and one possible reason for this might be the belief that souls continued to exist after death. As I mentioned in my previous book, there is no practical reasons for hunter-gatherers to bury their dead for reasons of sanitation. Tyler said that beliefs (such as animism) become religion once they are institutionalized through communal rituals. Burial ceremonies might be one such ritual.

Tyler believed that from animism arose a belief in an afterlife; that after death souls continued to exist. The deceased were both venerated and feared. It was believed that released souls could enter other living beings, i.e. possession. "From the belief in spirits or souls being loose in the world and capable of possessing living and inanimate beings, comes the viewpoint, according to Tyler, that all of nature is possessed or animated by these spirits. Some are good, and some are evil. From this comes the idea that spirits become

Gods and rule various aspects of nature." Over time a hierarchy of the Gods developed; some Gods more important and more powerful than others.

The Gods of early civilizations such as Sumeria and Egypt were very human-like in most respects; they enjoyed fine food and wine, they were passionate, they got married and had affairs, and they were often petty and self-centered. They were different from humans though in that they had superhuman powers and were immortal. Humans were created for the purpose of serving the Gods.

Evil was thought of as anything that negatively impacted humans. This included both natural evils such as earthquakes and famines and also personal calamities such as the death of a child or physical illness. When tragedies befell individuals or nations, it was felt to be the consequence of actions or inaction by the individuals or nations that caused it. Gods needed to be pleased and appeased, and this was done primarily through making sacrifices. Morality really wasn't involved here. The Gods were no more moral than the humans who served them.

There were, however, kind and beneficent Gods as well as cruel and selfish Gods. One of the earliest evil supernatural characters in literature was the demon Humbaba, the servant of the God Enlil. Humbaba is a character in the Sumerian epic poem "The Epic of Gilgamesh", which is perhaps the earliest piece of literature in existence today. It dates to 2100 BCE. In this poem Humbaba guarded the Cedar Forest where the Gods lived, a dark and foreboding place that was terrifying to humans. In the Sumerian religion there was a belief in an underworld, a realm of the dead. The guardians of the underworld were the God Nergal and his consort, the Goddess Ereshkigal.

The Egyptians, in contrast, believed that upon death there would be a personal judgment on how one lived their life; paradise was reserved for those whose life warranted it. The Egyptians also believed in an underworld for the dead called Duat. It was ruled by the God Osiris. There were a number of Gods in the Egyptian pantheon, and one is of particular interest to the subject of evil. Set (or Seth) was the lustful "God of disorder". His appearance is particularly noteworthy; he had a long curved snout, long ears or horns, reddish skin, and sometimes was portrayed with a forked tip on his tail. These are some physical characteristics that many centuries later became associated with Satan.

The Sumerian and Egyptian civilizations preceded the Israelites by many centuries. As I laid out in my book "Evolution and Syncretism of Religion", many of the most ancient Israelite narratives are very similar to the much older Mesopotamian stories, such as the great flood narrative. Just as there were supernatural beings in the Mesopotamian and Egyptian narratives, so were there in ancient Israelite narratives, particularly the book of Genesis which is in the Hebrew scriptures.

Supernatural Beings in the Bible

The early Israelite religion was not monotheistic; it was *henotheistic*. This means the Israelites worshiped (or at least were only supposed to worship) one God while not denying the existence of other Gods. Like many of the religions of the ancient near east, the Hebrew scriptures speak of a "divine council". This is an assembly of Gods over which a primary God presides. As I wrote in my last book, "When man was first created, Genesis 1:26 tells us that God said

'Let *us* make humankind in *our* image, according to *our* likeness'. Mankind is made in the likeness of *Gods*, not just the one God. After Adam eats of the forbidden tree God said 'See, the man has become like one of *us*, knowing good and evil; and now, he might reach out his hand and take also from the tree of life, and eat, and live forever.' (Genesis 3:22). Man, like the *Gods*, now knows the difference between good and evil and could also potentially live forever, like the *Gods*. In the story of the Tower of Babel, God said 'Come, let *us* go down, and confuse their language there, so that they will not understand one another's speech.' (Genesis 11:7). Again Yahweh is part of a group of *Gods*." (Vander Maas, 2017)

The concept of a divine council of Gods was prevalent throughout Canaan and Mesopotamia. The concept is also presented in the Hebrew scriptures as we just saw in the book of Genesis. "Psalm 82 of the Hebrew scriptures says 'God has taken his place in the divine council; in the midst of the Gods he holds judgment.' A heavenly council is also presented in the book of Job: 'One day the heavenly beings came to present themselves before the Lord, and Satan also came among them' (Job 1:6). Satan was presented as one of the beings in this divine council of supernatural beings.

In all of the religions of the ancient near east there were a variety of Gods and also other supernatural beings, such as angels. It is not clear what the criteria for being a "God" is as opposed to being another supernatural being. Many "Gods" were created by other Gods. It might be better to think of the supernatural beings as being on a continuum rather than being categorically different. Some Gods are superior to other Gods. The progeny of Gods who impregnated human women are inferior to full Gods. One might recall many of these individuals from Greek and Roman mythology, e.g. Perseus, Achilles and Orpheus. They are known as *demigods.*

One group of supernatural beings mentioned in Genesis are the *Nephilim.* In Genesis 6 it is stated that the "sons of God" were attracted to the female humans and bore children with them. Many exegetes believe the term "sons of God" refers to angels. The nephilim were the progeny of these relationships. "These were the heroes that were of old, warriors of renown." The nephilim are mentioned again in the book of Numbers (13:32-33). Moses sent spies into the land of Canaan: "There we saw the Nephilim (the Anakites come from the Nephilim); and to ourselves we seemed like grasshoppers, and so we seemed to them."

Angels are mentioned early on in the Hebrew scriptures:

- "He drove out the man; and at the east of the garden of Eden he placed the cherubim, and a sword flaming and turning to guard the way to the tree of life." Genesis 3:24

- "The two angels came to Sodom in the evening, and Lot was sitting in the gateway of Sodom. When Lot saw them, he rose to meet them, and bowed down with his face to the ground." Genesis 19:1

- "Then Abraham reached out his hand and took the knife to kill his son. But the angel of the Lord called to him from heaven, and said, 'Abraham, Abraham!' And he said, 'Here I am.' He said, 'Do not lay your hand on the boy or do anything to him; for now I know that you fear God, since you have not withheld your son, your only son, from me.'" Genesis 22: 10-12

- "The angel of the Lord appeared to him (Gideon) and said to him, 'The Lord is with you, you mighty warrior.'" Judges 6:12

Cherubim are mentioned several times in scripture. They frequently serve as guards, such as at the gates of paradise. Seraphim are another type of angel; they are mentioned just once in Isaiah (6:2-3). Most angels are anonymous. Only two are known by name: Gabriel is mentioned in the books of Daniel and Luke, and Michael the archangel (a title indicating authority over other angels) who is mentioned in the books of Jude, Daniel, and Revelation.

Two particular supernatural beings are important to a discussion of evil. One is Mashit, the "Destroyer". This angel is described by S.A. Meier in "The Dictionary of Deities and Demons in the Bible" as a "supernatural envoy from God assigned the task of annihilating large numbers of people". (Van Der Toorn, et al). He is mentioned in Exodus 12:23, 2 Samuel 24:16 and 1 Chronicles 21:15. Although the Destroyer's specialty is mass slaughter, the angel acts only on behalf of God.

The other important angel is Satan, the "Adversary". The term *satan* is used as a non-proper noun during the period of the divided kingdoms (900 to 600 BCE) to refer to someone who is an accuser, or adversary or trouble maker. The Hebrew term is used in 1 Sam 29:4; 2 Sam 19:17-24; 1 Kings 5:4; 11:14, 23, 25; Psalms 109:1-6.

"Satan" is first used as a proper noun in the book of Job. Ha-satan is the name of a heavenly being who is part of

God's council of deities and angels. The book of Job was written after the Babylonian exile during the Persian period-somewhere between 530 and 400 BCE. Ha-satan is skeptical about the faith and uprightness of Job. God allows Ha-satan to persecute Job to test his faith.

This story confronts the thorny issue of theodicy. The religion of the Israelites had become monotheistic, i.e. the belief that there existed only one God. Along with this belief come some philosophical dilemmas. With polytheism good came from good deities, and evil came from evil deities. With monotheism it follows that both good and bad come from the one God. The book of Job deals with the issue of why bad things happen to good people. Even though the Israelites believe in only one God, the Job story suggests that there still might be supernatural beings who have an influence on bad things happening in the world.

When you think about it, there really is not a significant difference in the overall conception of deities between religions considered by many as polytheistic (such as Hinduism) and monotheistic religions. Hindus believe in one supreme God known as Brahman who is formless, limitless and eternal. From the supreme God emanate lesser Gods. Most Christians also believe in one God from whom other supernatural beings emanate.

Also written during the Persian period were First and Second Chronicles. When originally written, this was a single book that retold the Israelite history all the way from Adam and Eve through the events covered in 1-2 Kings and 1-2 Samuel. It is a revisionist history reflecting the beliefs of that time period. Whereas in 2 Samuel 24:1 God is said to be angry and tells King David to complete a census of the Israelite people, in 1 Chronicles 21:1 it is Satan who incites

David to do the census. During the Persian period Satan has become an actual entity who, although he causes trouble, is a comrade of God.

Also during the Persian period is the book of Zechariah, which primarily describes eight dreams or visions. The fourth vision's setting is a gathering of the divine council (as begins the book of Job). Like in the book of Job, Satan is present and serves the role as "accuser". Satan is a member of God's council.

Evolution of Satan

And so originally the word "satan" was a Hebrew common noun meaning "adversary" or "opponent". It was during the Persian period (540-330 BCE) that it became a proper name for a member of God's council. How did Satan then become the epitome of evil that we find in the New Testament?

One important influence was the Persian religion Zoroastrianism. Cyrus, the king of Persia, was a hero to the Israelite people, for he defeated the Babylonians (the great enemy who had destroyed the Jewish temple and exiled the Jewish people). Zoroastrianism was a monotheistic religion; they believed in only one true God, a creator God named Ahura Mazda. However, like with the Israelites, they believed that Ahura Mazda was the leader of a divine council of other lesser divinities. The Persians believed that evil did not come from God but rather from a separate, evil being called Ahriman. The religion taught that there was a constant struggle between Ahura Mazda and Ahriman, i.e. between good and evil. Wray and Mobley (2005) describe Ahriman as "the destructive personification (and creator) of evil, the

35

harbinger of death, disease, and lies." They also suggest that Ahriman may have significantly influenced the concept of Satan in the books of Job, Zechariah and Chronicles.

Zoroastrians believed that those who lived lives devoted to good deeds would enter a paradise, while those who engaged in evil would be banished to the torments of hell. I need to emphasize here that the Israelites had no concept of heaven and hell at this point of history. They generally believed in a place called Sheol where all would go after death, whether one was good or evil. The Zoroastrian hell was a horrifying place. It was described in the Vision of Arda Viraf (written between 226 and 641 CE):

I saw the greedy jaws of hell: the most frightful pit, descending, in a very narrow, fearsome crevice and in darkness so murky that I was forced to feel my way, amid such stench that all who inhaled the air, struggled, staggered, and fell, and in such confinement that existence seemed impossible. Each one thought: 'I am alone.'

I saw also, the soul of a man, the skin of whose head was being flayed... who in the world had slain a pious man. I saw the soul of a man into whose mouth they poured continually the menstrual discharge of a woman while he cooked and ate his own child... 'While in the world,' I was told that 'that wicked man had intercourse with a menstruating woman.' (Hopfe and Woodward, 2009).

Also important during the Persian period was the development of a genre of literature known as *apocalyptic*. Zoroastrianism also likely had a significant influence on this genre. Apocalyptic literature is concerned primarily with the war between good and evil, with the present age being characterized by evil. In the future, divine intervention will occur which will overthrow the enemies of God, and an age of righteousness will be implemented. Zoroastrians taught that the present age was a time of crisis and that a great Savior would restore goodness. That savior would be born of a virgin, would bring about the resurrection of the dead, and would make humankind immortal. Hopfe and Woodward (2009) remind us "pre-exilic biblical books have no mention of a resurrection of the body, little concern for life after death in either heaven or hell, no reference to God's plan for bringing the earth to an end, only an occasional mention of angels, and no word about a day of judgment. Each of these themes, which were part of the teachings of Zoroastrianism, developed in Judaism after the exile, and each had become a vital part of the religion by the time of Jesus."

A very important time period for the development of the character of Satan was the Intertestimental Period from 200 BCE to 200 CE, the time period between the Old and New Testaments. This was the period that apocalyptic literature developed and became popular. Although not a part of the Hebrew scriptures, an important writing at this time was The First Book of Enoch. I discussed previously in this chapter the nephilim in the book of Genesis; they were giants who were the offspring of angels and human women. The story of the *benay elohim* is told in Enoch. These are the "sons of God" who were the fathers of the nephilim. They also are referred to as "the Watchers" in Enoch. These were angels appointed by God to watch over the universe. Two hundred of them decided to descend to earth to mate with the human women.

There are three references to the Watchers in the book of Daniel in the Hebrew scriptures. Daniel is an apocalyptic book believed to have taken its final form around 167 BCE;

it was the latest written book to be included in the Hebrew canon. The book is the only full fledged example of apocalypticism in the Hebrew scriptures and focuses on the current evils which are the result of domination by foreign governments. It promises deliverance by God in the future. Angels or "watchers" do not have particular significance in the writing, but it is interesting that "watchers" are mentioned in that it shows they were known in the culture at that time, and they are important in that they were part of the legend in the development of Satan.

The "Watchers" are important in the book of Enoch. They provide an explanation for evil in the world and describe a leader of these fallen angels.

The Watcher angels- as they are now called- have a leader, whose name is Semyaza. The names of the Devil vary, particularly in the Apocalyptic period: he is Belial, Mastema, Azazel, Satanail, Sammael, Demyaza, or Satan. These names have different origins, and the beings they denote differ in their origins and functions one from another. But gradually they coalesce. The Devil becomes a spiritual being personifying the origin and essence of evil: there can be only one Devil. Previous studies that have concentrated exclusively upon the name of Satan have obscured this fact. As the Devil has many names in different religions, so he has many names within the Judeo-Christian tradition itself. Of all these names, that of Satan became the greatest. (Russell, 1977).

Interestingly, the devil is named "Azazel" throughout most of the book of Enoch, but the name changes to "Satan" in the later chapters. "By the time the final chapters were written (in the first century BCE), apparently the name 'Satan,' rather than 'Azazel,' had become the popular designation for the Evil One." (Wray and Mobley, 2005)

Also written during this time period was the book of Jubilees, written between 160 and 140 BCE. This is a re-telling of the stories of Genesis and Exodus from the viewpoint of that later time period. Instead of God being responsible for some questionable deeds, it is an evil one that is responsible, usually referred to as "Mastema". In Genesis it is written that God tells Abraham to sacrifice his son Isaac; in Jubilees it is Mastema that tells Abraham to do this act. In this book it is written that God allowed Mastema to retain a tenth of his gang to continue their troublemaking, with the remainder being sent to "the place of condemnation". Later on in the book of Jubilees the name of the evil one changes from Mastema to Satan, again likely reflecting that over time the name "Satan" won out over other names.

Another apocalyptic work of the time period was the Testaments of the Twelve Patriarchs; these were writings purportedly from the twelve sons of Jacob (the son of Isaac and grandson of Abraham). The testament of the firstborn, Reuben, contains additional myth about the Watchers and is believed to have later contributed to lore about witches. In this writing the Watchers do not physically impregnate human women but rather supernaturally impregnate them while they are having intercourse with their husbands, i.e. they are an incubus. (Russell, 1977).

There were many writings during the Intertestimental Period that contributed to the burgeoning folklore about Satan. One of these was "The First and Second Books of Adam and Eve: the Conflict with Satan". The story explains that Satan and the other angels were created before humans. Adam was created in the image of God, and so the angel Michael commands that the angels worship the humans. Satan because of pride refuses; he is envious of humans, i.e. that God is preferential to humans. God in anger banishes Satan and the angels who follow him from heaven.

Satan in the New Testament

To summarize up to this point, the word *satan* started off as a common noun in Hebrew for someone who is an adversary or opponent. During the Persian period it became a proper name for a member of God's council in heaven, a being who served as somewhat of an instigator. During the Intertestimental Period Satan evolved to become the being responsible for evil. In early Israelite monotheism God was known to be responsible for everything- both good and evil. Likely due to influences of Persian Zoroastrianism, a number of evil beings coalesced into the fallen angel Satan, who became the anthropomorphized epitome of evil. And so in the history of morality supernatural beings were the ones responsible for good and evil in the world.

The Synoptic gospels (Matthew, Mark and Luke) make mention of Satan. The most well-known story about Jesus and Satan was when Jesus fasted in the wilderness for forty days and forty nights (reminiscent of Moses and the Israelites wandering in the wilderness for forty years). It is mentioned briefly in the book of Mark (1:12-13), but is dealt with in some detail in Matthew (4:1-11) and Luke (4:1-13). "The devil" tempts Jesus to turn a stone into bread (reminiscent of God providing manna to the Israelites in the wilderness) to demonstrate his power, to throw himself off a high place to show that he would be supernaturally protected, and to worship the devil who offered to make him king of all the kingdoms of the world if he were to do this.

One might surmise from these synoptic gospels that Satan was a supernatural being that literally interacted with Jesus. The gospel of John, however, also discusses these temptations of Jesus, but in John it is not Satan who does the tempting but crowds of people. John 6:15 says that Jesus realized the people "were about to come and take him by force to make him king". John 6:30-31 states that the people requested that Jesus make manna from heaven to show his power, as God did for the Israelites in the wilderness. In John 7:1-5, it is Jesus' own brothers who insincerely request of Jesus to show his powers to be recognized and worshiped.

Did the New Testament writers conceive of Satan as a supernatural being who is the embodiment of evil, or is Satan a metaphor for evil? In Luke 22:3 it is written that "Satan entered into Judas called Iscariot". Was Judas possessed? Was Satan responsible for the betrayal and Jesus' subsequent crucifixion? In the gospel of Matthew (16:23) Jesus refers to his disciple Peter as "satan", ironically for trying to prevent the thing that Judas was complicit in causing, i.e. the Passion. Certainly he did not think Peter was possessed. In this instance it would appear that "satan" is being used in the generic sense to mean "obstacle".

The use of the term "satan" by the apostle Paul also appears to be referring to an "obstructor", one who hinders the work of the church. A good example is a passage from Paul's letter to the Romans, the writing of Paul that is probably the best summary of Pauline theology:

I urge you, brothers and sisters, to keep an eye on those who cause dissensions and offenses, in opposition to the teaching that you have learned; avoid them. For such people do not serve our Lord Christ, but their own appetites, and by smooth talk and flattery they deceive the hearts of the simple-minded. For while your obedience is known to all, so that I rejoice over you, I want you to be wise in what is good and guileless in what is evil. The God of peace will shortly crush Satan under your feet. (Romans 16: 17-20).

In the words of Wray and Mobley (2005), "Satan is understood to be symbolic of those who seek to disrupt and scandalize the Roman Christian community."

Also in the Synoptic gospels (but not at all in the gospel of John), Jesus as part of his healing ministry was said to cast out demons. Religious scholar Reza Aslan (2013) maintains that exorcists were common in Palestine at that time. Illnesses were viewed as the result of either divine judgment or demon possession. Aslan writes "Jesus's status as an exorcist and miracle worker may seem unusual, even absurd, to modern skeptics, but it did not deviate greatly from the standard expectation of exorcists and miracle workers in first-century Palestine. Whether Greek, Roman, Jewish, or Christian, all peoples in the ancient Near East viewed magic and miracle as a standard facet of their world."

The book in the New Testament that is most pertinent to the topic of Satan is the apocalyptic book of Revelation. This was a controversial writing from the beginning and almost did not make it into the New Testament cannon. It was written by John of Patmos almost a century after the birth of Christ. The author shares a series of visions he's had which depict the conflict between good and evil. Biblical scholars most frequently believe that John is writing about the oppression that was occurring at the hands of the Romans, and that the "whore of Babylon" in the book is a reference to

Rome. In chapters 12-24 Satan is portrayed as the epitome of evil and the archenemy of God. John describes a cosmic battle between the forces of good (God, the saints, and the angels) and the forces of evil (Satan and his demons).

Satan after the New Testament

Apocalypse as a genre continued to be popular in the first centuries of the common era. Writings included the Apocalypse of Peter, the Apocalypse of Paul, and the Apocalypse of the Virgin. In these writings the concept of "hell" becomes more developed. In the Hebrew scriptures there is no mention of a hell. All of the dead, whether living a righteous or an evil life, went to a place called Sheol. The Hebrew scriptures do talk about a heaven, but that is the place for God and the angels, not a place for humans to go after death. Like the concept of Satan, the concept of hell took centuries to evolve.

During the Intertestimental Period the idea of judgment after death developed, i.e. that no longer would everyone just automatically go to Sheol, but that the righteous would be rewarded, and the evil would be punished. The New Testament makes references to Hades and Gehenna. The reference to Gehenna comes from a garbage dump outside of Jerusalem where child sacrifice had taken place. The synoptic gospels make mention of a place of punishment for sinners (although the name "hell" is never used), and Paul makes no mention of such a place. Punishment for sinners does not appear to be a part of Pauline theology; sinners who reject Christ would simply die, while those who accepted Christ would experience resurrection after death.

A writing that greatly contributed to the lore about hell was Dante Alighieri's "The Divine Comedy" which was completed in 1320. This three-part epic poem describes hell in "Inferno", which is part one. Purgatory, and heaven in "Paradiso" are also described. Although a work of fiction, it had great influence on Christian beliefs. The protagonist, who is Dante himself, is guided through nine levels of hell by the Roman poet, Virgil. Below Purgatory is Limbo.

First Circle (Limbo)

- This level contains the unbaptized and virtuous pagans.

Second Circle (Lust)

- The lustful are punished with the constant buffeting of strong winds.

Third Circle (Gluttony)

- Gluttons are condemned to live in a stinking garbage heap.

Fourth Circle (Greed)

- Misers are punished with enormous weights which they strain to roll against each other.

Fifth Circle (Wrath)

- The angry fight each other viciously in a horrible swamp of the river Styx, while the sullen lie beneath the waters where there is no joy.

Sixth Circle (Heresy)

- Those with heretical beliefs are trapped in burning graves for eternity.

Seventh Circle (Violence)

- Murderers and tyrants are immersed in a river of boiling blood and fire. Those who committed or attempted suicide are transformed into thorny trees and then are fed upon by hideous clawed birds. This level also contains the blasphemers, sodomites, and usurers (those who lend money at unreasonable rates).

Eight Circle (Fraud)

- This level includes those who exploit others, fortune tellers, astrologers, popes who kept money for themselves that belonged to God (Dante listed specific popes), corrupt politicians, hypocrites and thieves.

Ninth Circle (Treachery)

- This level is reserved for traitors (Judas Iscariot is there).

Center of Hell

- It is here that we have Satan who is trapped in a frozen lake. The portrayal of Satan here is somewhat surprising as he is presented as a pathetic and weak creature.

Satan is presented much differently in the other later writing that greatly influenced Christian beliefs, i.e. John Milton's

"Paradise Lost". This epic poem was written in 1667. Following a failed rebellion against God, Satan and his followers are banished from heaven and cast into a fiery lake. Satan and his companions crawl out of the fire and build a palace named Pandemonium on the side of a volcano. From there they plot and scheme. Satan is a powerful creature with an army who is able to fly back and forth between hell and earth.

The blending of contributions from both of these literary works with Biblical writings and earlier non-canonical apoc-alyptic writings have created an image of Satan and hell that is still prevalent to this day. The physical image that has developed of Satan comes from a number of sources. Having horns and a tail is reminiscent of Habayu, the Canaanite demon. Red skin may have come from the wicked Egyptian god, Set. The Greek god Poseidon's trident may have become Satan's pitchfork, and the Greek god Pan's appearance as half-man and half-goat also contributed.

The concepts of Satan, demons, and condemnation to hell have been important and prevalent beliefs since the Intertes-timental Period in regards to evil. Although belief in Satan and hell have been on the downswing since the Enlighten-ment, many Christians still believe that Satan is the reason for evil in the world. A 2005 Baylor University religion sur-vey suggested that "roughly 58 percent of Americans abso-lutely believe in Satan while slightly fewer (48%) believe in demons. (Stark, 2008)

A later survey in 2007 by this same group probed this topic further. That survey found that 43% of its respondents agreed with "Most evil in the world is caused by the devil" and 89% of its respondents agreed with "Most evil in the world is caused by mankind." The reason these percentages did not add up to 100% or less is that many people endorsed both the devil and mankind as being responsible for most of the evil in the world. It also found that 25% of the respondents believed that "Human nature is basically evil." The survey broke this down in terms of denomination, gender, race, and education.

For those who agree that most evil in the world is caused by the devil, here are some statistical breakdowns:

Conservative Protestants	73%
Roman Catholics	38%
Liberal Protestants	34%
Atheists	0%
Women	47%
Men	39%
African Americans	70%
Whites	40%
High school education or less	50%
Those who attended graduate school	26%

Religious Law

Satan was one concept that was important in the Christian conception of evil. Also important was the creation of laws. During the time of the Hebrew patriarchs (Abraham, Isaac, Jacob) religious expression primarily consisted of making sacrifices. During the time of Abraham a new requirement was made for him and his male descendants, i.e. to be circumcised. During prehistorical times humans lived first in *bands* (25 to 100 family members who were hunter-gatherers), and then later larger groups called *tribes*. You may recall that during the time of Moses the Israelite people were made up of twelve tribes. Small groups of family members do not need laws, but larger groups of non-kin and strangers do need laws to keep order. The Hebrew book of Exodus tells us that God gave laws to the Israelites to follow. They were conveyed through Moses and began with the famous Ten Commandments. Many other laws also were given to the Israelites, and these are described in the books of Exodus, Leviticus, Numbers and Deuteronomy. The first five books of the Hebrew Bible are known as the Torah. Torah in Hebrew means law.

I describe in my previous book "Evolution and Syncretism of Religion" how Hebrew law was very similar to Mesopotamian law codes, such as the Code of Hammurabi, written many centuries earlier. As civilizations developed, there was a need for laws to be written to keep order. Many of the Hebrew laws were for this purpose, e.g. not to kill, not to steal, etc. Other laws were for religious reasons, i.e. to be faithful to the god, Yahweh. Other laws were for perceived sanitation and health reasons, e.g. not to have sexual relations with women who are menstruating, how to handle people with leprosy, etc. For many people religion became primarily duty to follow law. During Jesus' time, this was the main emphasis of the Pharisees, although for the Sadducees sacrifice continued to be the primary focus. For many individuals to this day religion and morality primarily involves following laws.

The Axial Age

A revolution in thinking occurred during the time period that has come to be known as the "Axial Age", a term coined by German philosopher and psychiatrist, Karl Jaspers. In the beginning of this book I have included several versions of what has come to be known as the "golden rule". This has been articulated by numerous spiritual leaders from numerous religions. This philosophy is a product of the Axial Age. The time period of the axial age was from 800 BCE to 200 BCE. Religion and moral development took a giant leap forward during this period. Religion had grown from making sacrifices to please the gods, to laws that made societies work, to concerns about others, i.e. a focus on *love*. There was a new focus on being other-centered rather than just self-centered.

Jaspers listed what he saw as four critical stages in the evolution of man, and the third of these stages was the axial revolution. The stages are:

1. The genesis of speech, the use of tools, and the use of fire "through which he first became man".

2. The establishment of the first ancient civilizations.

3. The Axial Period "through which, spiritually, he [man] unfolded his full human potentialities".

4. The scientific-technological age.

Now for the first time morality became important in religion. As I think I've demonstrated, morality long predated religion and I would say was present in even other species that predated humans and in other species that are present today.

Animals have shown care and concern for others even if not in their short-term best interests, including to animals of other species. Animals other than humans have shown they have the capacity for empathy, sympathy and altruism.

Early religion was very self-centered. The focus was on pleasing and appeasing gods completely for self-interest, i.e. to decrease pain and suffering and to increase wealth and prosperity. Sacrifices were made to gods for help for them-selves, not for non-kin or those seen as the "other". Unfortunately, much of religion even to this day seems to be only to serve self-interests. One example would be so called "prosperity theology" which teaches that financial prosperity and good health is what results from faith in God. We serve God because God will reward us for it.

Another example of the self-serving nature of many religions is the belief that faith in God will present rewards not in this life but in the afterlife. The sole focus for many is to gain personal salvation. For many Christians there is not love for the "other" but only love for the self and those seen as of "our kind". For example, I have heard from several people who professed to be "Christian" the desire that people they perceive as evil to not have a "conversion", rather preferring to see such people suffer for eternity in hell.

The Old Testament prophets during the Axial Age took the emphasis off from sacrifice and the following of laws. They stressed justice and concern for the less fortunate, e.g. the poor and widows. I included this quote from the prophet Amos (chapter 5) in my last book, and I think it bears repeating here:

I hate, I despise your festivals,
and I take no delight in your solemn assemblies.
Even though you offer me your burnt offerings and grain
offerings,
I will not accept them;
and the offerings of well-being of your fatted animals
I will not look upon.
Take away from me the noise of your songs;
I will not listen to the melody of your harps.
But let justice roll down like waters,
and righteousness like an ever-flowing stream.

Jesus criticized the pharisees for their legalism, i.e. the focus on following laws to the letter of the law rather than keeping in mind the reasons the laws were made in the first place. A good example is "keeping the Sabbath holy". Why did God make this rule? The word "sabbath" comes from the Hebrew word *shabbat* which means "to rest". The reason for this law (as explained in Exodus 23:12 and Deuteronomy 5:12-15) is to give respite from work for all people including slaves and animals, i.e. that it is a requirement for compassion and care of others. It is a call for care to others. Legalists focus on the law itself and lose sight for the reason (compassion). Jesus was confronted by pharisees for doing acts on the Sabbath, such as healing others. Jesus asked the pharisees "Does the Law command us to do good on Sabbath days or do harm—to save life or destroy it?" (Luke 6:9).

Jesus summarizes all of the Jewish laws as really being at heart to be about loving God and loving others. I believe that this is the heart of morality. To be "good", to be moral, is about not being self-centered but rather is about loving God and others. It is about justice and about being fair. It is about following the "Golden Rule", although I would make a small adjustment to the saying as it is most commonly expressed. Rather than doing to others what *I* would want done to me, I would say it is about doing to others what *they* would want done. The original formulation of the golden rule still has some degree of self-centeredness; if it is what I would want, then it must be what others would want as well. So for example, if I am deciding on a Christmas present for a loved one, I need to consider what they would want rather than thinking that if I want it, they should want it too.

I agree with philosopher Joseph Fletcher (1966) that "only one thing is intrinsically good, namely love: nothing else at all." Morality is all about love- the type of love expressed by the Greek word *agape*. This type of love is non-reciprocal, giving love. It is the love of "neighbor" we are encouraged by the Bible to have. It is explained well in the Gospel of Luke (6:32-35) by Jesus:

If you love those who love you, what credit is that to you? For even sinners love those who love them. If you do good to those who do good to you, what credit is that to you? For even sinners do the same. If you lend to those from whom you hope to receive, what credit is that to you? Even sinners lend to sinners, to receive as much again. But love your enemies, do good, and lend, expecting nothing in return. Your reward will be great, and you will be children of the Most High; for he is kind to the ungrateful and the wicked.

I also like the definition of love given by the psychiatrist M. Scott Peck (1978): Love is "the will to extend one's self for the purpose of nurturing one's own or another's spiritual growth". *Agape* is different from two other types of love: *philia* which is friendship love, and *eros* which is romantic love. Both of these types of love are selective; we don't have this type of love for everyone. They are only for the ones we love in a romantic way or those we choose to devote time to in order to develop friendships. These are relationships that are conditional; we expect something in return in these relationships. *Agape* is about an unconditional love.

Probably the most common Biblical passage to be used at Christian weddings is 1 Corinthians 13:1-7. Many people believe this refers to *eros*, but it is actually a letter written to the church in Corinth by the apostle Paul and refers to *agape:*

If I speak in the tongues of men or of angels, but do not have love, I am only a resounding gong or a clanging cymbal. If I have the gift of prophecy and can fathom all mysteries and all knowledge, and if I have a faith that can move mountains, but do not have love, I am nothing. If I give all I possess to the poor and give over my body to hardship that I may boast, but do not have love, I gain nothing.

Love is patient, love is kind. It does not envy, it does not boast, it is not proud. It does not dishonor others, it is not self-seeking, it is not easily angered, it keeps no record of wrongs. Love does not delight in evil but rejoices with the truth. It always protects, always trusts, always hopes, always perseveres.

In the introduction to this book I briefly discussed some of the disputes in the philosophical field of ethics. One controversy involves whether behaviors should be considered moral based on consequences or whether they should be based on a principle. Thus one group are called "consequentialists" and the other "nonconsequentialists". I would consider myself a nonconsequentialist in that I believe the principle of love makes a behavior moral. Anything done out of agape is automatically moral in my view. This would

53

include behaviors generally considered not moral, such as lying. If it is done to protect another person and is done from love, it is not immoral. I also would consider myself a consequentialist in that I believe that all behaviors done out of love *inevitably* contribute to evolution of humanity and the universe. More about this later on in the book.

Another controversy involves whether morality is absolute or relative. In other words, are there absolute rights and wrongs. I believe in moral absolutes, and again it involves love. Everything done in love is moral, and behaviors done out of self-centeredness that harm others are immoral. Many might consider me a moral relativist in that I would not say that killing is always wrong, stealing is always wrong, abortion is always wrong, lying is always wrong, etc. However, I maintain I am a moral absolutist in that I believe that everything done truly out of love is moral. Again, some of these ideas will be further explored as the book progresses.

Chapter Two

Evil as

Psychopathology

I would like to begin chapter two by returning to the topics of Satan, demons, possession and exorcism. During the time period of Jesus, exorcisms were a common occurrence, and Jesus participated in casting out demons and curing illnesses. The "possessed" individuals were not portrayed as evil but as suffering illnesses. The incidences described in the synoptic gospels of Jesus casting out demons had the intention of demonstrating Jesus' power and authority over these demons, not about the power that Satan has over the world, which is the way Satan was portrayed centuries later. The symptoms identified in the exorcism stories in the synoptic gospels are almost exclusively physical, e.g. loss of speech, hearing or sight and convulsions. Jesus was essentially a healer.

"The number of people reportedly possessed by demons in early modern Europe certainly reached into the thousands... Belief in possession by demons was deeply ingrained in early modern European culture." (Levack, 2013). So what were the symptoms that led people to believe that someone was possessed at that time? Levack said symptoms could be divided into those that were physiological (such as seizures and muscular rigidity) and those that involved changes in speech, personality, or moral conduct. These symptoms may have been the result of psychosis, head injuries, or brain tumors. Back in that day illnesses and psychopathology were labeled as evil. I believe just the opposite and will try to make this point in this chapter: evil is psychopathology.

A parallel and related phenomenon to demon possession was witchcraft. "Today most of us think of witches as a kind of independent magical species- a folk superstition, not part of the Christian scheme. And for the thousand years or so that Catholics ran Christianity, the church agreed: witchcraft officially didn't exist during the Middle Ages. But as soon as Protestantism emerged, so did alleged witches and witch hunts" (Andersen, 2017). The Reverend Cotton Mather published "Memorable Providences, Relating to Witchcrafts and Possessions". The Salem witchcraft trials became an epidemic. "In four months more than two hundred trials produced dozens of guilty verdicts, mostly of women, and at least twenty witches and sorcerers (and two satanic pet dogs) were executed. A few others died in jail. The total population of the towns of Salem and Andover was only 2,400" (Andersen, 2017).

"In the past four decades researchers have suggested that demoniacs were afflicted by, among other things, bipolar disorder, catatonic schizophrenia, epilepsy, palsy, Tourette's syndrome, chorea (a nervous disorder marked by a spasmodic movement of the limbs), ergot poisoning, anorexia, and trance disorders. The most popular of these explanations is commonly referred to as multiple personality disorder, which is one of many aetiological stepchildren of hysteria" (Levack, 2013).

What is evil?

I believe the essence of morality is the philosophy found in the "golden rule", a philosophy found in all the major religions since the Axial Age. It is a philosophy against self-centeredness. It is a philosophy that exhorts us to love others. Life should not be about just finding pleasure for ourselves, gaining as much money and possessions as we can, and having concern for only our own happiness and the avoidance of pain. I think we all struggle to one degree or another with selfishness and self-centeredness, but there are degrees in how much this is manifested in individuals. Some people are more moral than others.

Sigmund Freud talked about the *id* as being the most primitive part of our personality. It is dominated by the *pleasure principle* whose goal is to maximize pleasure and to minimize pain. It seeks to satisfy basic desires, urges and needs. "I want what I want when I want it." As young children mature they develop an *ego*; the id is kept in check by the ego which follows the *reality principle,* the development of reason and good sense. Also, according to Freud, the individual will develop a *superego*, which is a moral conscience. This is heavily influenced by our parents and other important people in our lives.

Individuals vary in terms of their degree of emotional and moral development. Some people's degree of control over id impulses is relatively minimal; these people care about nothing but themselves and their own happiness. Psychoanalysis has also addressed people who have overly punitive superegos; they are people who are overly guilt-ridden and can't forgive themselves for mistakes. On one end of the morality continuum are Stalin and Hitler whose self-centeredness led to the deaths of millions. On the other end of the continuum was Mother Theresa, who completely dedicated her life to the service of the downtrodden.

The term "evil" has often been used to refer to people who are morally sinister- people who do such awful things that they are beyond the bounds of what would be considered normal. We usually don't consider behaviors such as white lies, shoplifting, adultery and drunk driving as "evil", although we may consider them "bad" or "a sin". On the other hand, committing genocide, drowning one's own baby, and sadistic torture most would consider "evil".

When I speak of "evil", I am referring only to *moral* evils as opposed to *natural* evils such as earthquakes, tidal waves, or even cancer, which I do not consider as "evil" at all. These are "acts of God", and I don't believe that God commits evil. God is love, and evil is the opposite of love. I would consider myself both a *consequentialist* and a *non-consequentialist*. I am a *non-consequentialist* in that I believe that any act committed out of love is moral. Others believe this as well, perhaps the most well-known being Joseph Fletcher (1966), as well as Emil Brunner, Dietrich Bonhoeffer, Reinhold Niebuhr, and Paul Tillich. Fletcher states that "only one 'thing' is intrinsically good; namely, love: nothing else at all." Consequently, malice is intrinsically evil. Fletcher also points out that love and justice are the same. We cannot be loving if we deprive justice. Justice is love in action.

Fletcher points out that legalism has predominated in Christian thought despite Jesus' and Paul's teachings. Jesus was asked by a lawyer about which of the commandments in the law was the greatest. Jesus responded with "'You shall love the Lord your God with all your heart, and with all your soul, and with all your mind'. This is the greatest and first commandment. And a second is like it: 'You shall love your neighbor as yourself.' On these two commandments hang all the law and the prophets." In other words, the only purpose for rules and laws is to show love to God and to others. And yet still perhaps a majority of people feel that to be moral they need to be primarily rule followers rather than to act in love. They miss the forest for the trees.

I said that I believe I am both a non-consequentialist as well as a consequentialist. The reason that I believe I am also a consequentialist is my belief that when we act in love, the consequences ultimately will be further evolution of God's kingdom, the universe. Love leads to evolution, while self-centeredness and malice leads to regression. Love leads to growth and progress. Evolution is about growth and progress.

You may say in response to this that by acting in your own selfish, individual best interests (as Ayn Rand might advocate), you are furthering your own progress and evolution. That may be true. However, often in pursuing our own self-interests without regard for others, we hinder the growth and progress of others. Consequently this is an impediment to the growth of the greater good. We are used to focusing on ourselves primarily, and when we extend concern for others it is to our family- then perhaps to extended family- then perhaps to our immediate community- then perhaps to the larger society- then perhaps to our whole species- then perhaps to the biosphere (the global ecological system that integrates all living things). A prevailing view is that we do better when we "look after number one". I don't think that's true. I think that in the long run we all do better if we all look out for each other. The more extravagantly we sow love, the greater the yield.

I first ran across a little story about a wave in a book by Mitch Albom entitled *Tuesdays with Morrie* (1997). I am not sure where the story originated. It really had an impact on me.

I heard a nice little story the other day," Morrie says. He closes his eyes for a moment and I wait.

"Okay. The story is about a little wave, bobbing along in the ocean, having a grand old time. He's enjoying the wind and the fresh air- until he notices the other waves in front of him, crashing against the shore.

"'My God, this is terrible,' the wave says. 'Look what's going to happen to me!"

"Then along comes another wave. It sees the first wave, looking grim, and it says to him, 'Why do you look so sad?'

"The first wave says, 'You don't understand! We're all going to crash! All of us waves are going to be nothing! Isn't it terrible?'

"The second wave says, 'No, you don't understand. You're not a wave, you're part of the ocean.

Rather than focusing on how big a wave we can be, or how big a splash we can make, I think our focus should be on how we can best improve the quality of the water.

The Bell Curve

What does it mean to be "normal?" As a psychologist and neuropsychologist my main job is to assess normality from psychopathology. A neuropsychologist is a clinical psychologist who has additional specialized training in assessing neurological disorders such as dementia, various congenital conditions, and sequelae of brain injuries and concussions. It is concerned with the behavioral expression of brain dysfunction.

Normality does not mean healthy or preferable; rather is refers to what is typical or most common. A visual representation of a normal distribution is something called the "bell curve". It is shown below:

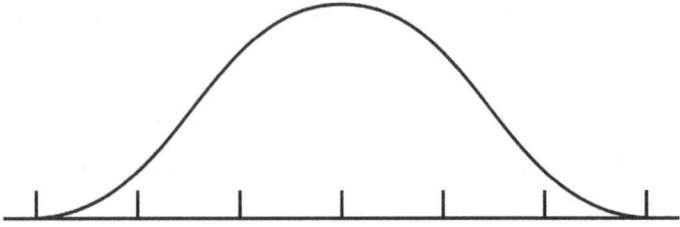

If we look at natural phenomenon, this is how data will arrange itself. Examples of this "natural phenomenon" include the length of elephant's trunks, how fast 30 year old women can run the 100-yard dash, intelligence, and degree of self-centeredness. So, with the example of the length of elephant trunks, most trunks will have an "average" length; extremely long trunks and extremely short trunks are rare. They would be at the "tails" of the above bell curve.

A synonym for "mean" is "average". If I am teaching a graduate psychology class and I want to know the average age in the class, I would add up all the ages of the participants and then divide by the number of students. This would give me the "mean". If I had a large enough sample size, I could figure out what the mean length of elephant trunks is. There is a statistical formula for figuring out something called "the standard deviation". This is a description of the amount of spread in a population. In a normal distribution 68.27 percent of all cases will fall in the interval between one standard deviation below the mean and one standard deviation above the mean. 95 percent of all cases will fall between two standard deviations, and 99.7 percent of all cases will fall between three standard deviations from the mean.

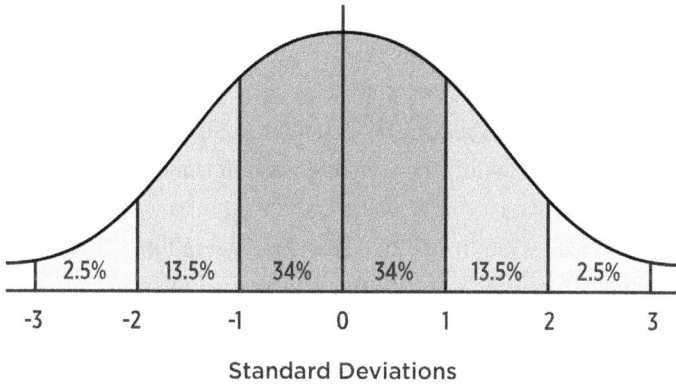

| 2.5% | 13.5% | 34% | 34% | 13.5% | 2.5% |

-3   -2   -1   0   1   2   3

Standard Deviations

Let's use the construct of *intelligence* as an example. If we are using a particular test of intelligence, the Wechsler Adult Intelligence Scale, we will be using a mean of 100 and a standard deviation of 15. That would mean 68.27 of people in the general population will have an IQ score between 85 and 115. If you are one standard deviation above the mean you will be at the 84th percentile, at two standard deviations above the mean you will be at the 98th percentile, and if you are three standard deviations from the mean you will be at the 99.9 percentile. If you are one standard deviation below the mean you will be at the 16th percentile, and at two standard deviations below the mean you will be at the 2nd percentile, and at three standard deviations below the mean at the .1th percentile.

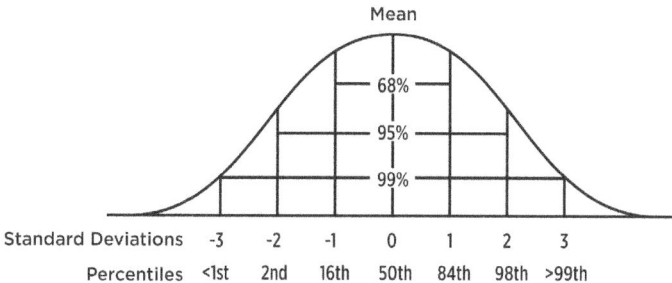

	Mean	
	68%	
	95%	
	99%	

| Standard Deviations | -3 | -2 | -1 | 0 | 1 | 2 | 3 |
| Percentiles | <1st | 2nd | 16th | 50th | 84th | 98th | >99th |

Generally what is considered "average" is one and one-half standard deviations from the mean, which would characterize 86 percent of the population as "average". Seven percent of the population would be considered abnormally low, and seven percent would be considered abnormally high, whatever construct it is that we are interested in. A more strict criteria would be to use two standard deviations; this would include 95 percent of individuals as being "average".

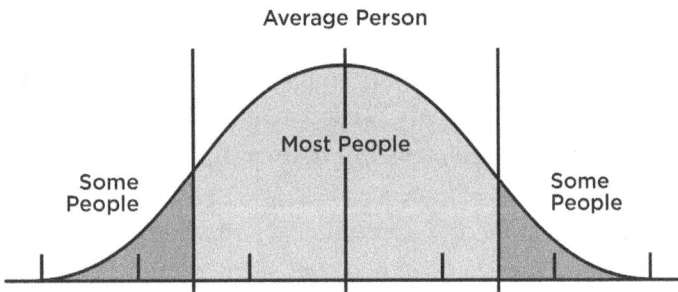

Average Person

Most People

Some People

Some People

The Diagnostic and Statistical Manual of Mental Disorders (DSM-5) (2013) is the major source used by clinicians and researchers to diagnose and classify mental disorders. One of the major differences between the fourth edition and the latest fifth edition is the move from putting mental disorders into distinct categories and instead to think of disorders as being on a continuum. For example, in DSM-IV substance *abuse* disorders were separate from substance *dependence* disorders, while in DSM-V *substance use disorders* combines the two and asks the clinician to designate if the disorder is mild, moderate or severe. In DSM-IV there are different categories of autistic disorders, while in DSM-V there is but one "Autistic Spectrum Disorder", and the clinician is again to determine the degree of severity.

Many constructs I believe are on a continuum rather than belonging to discreet categories. As far as other mental health conditions, many people have symptoms of depression, anxiety, ADHD, etc. The question is when it meets a level to warrant a diagnosis and treatment. Morality, I believe, is also on a continuum. It is not a matter of being either good or bad- it is to what degree. At one extreme are those who are so self-centered that they will do <u>anything</u> if it benefits themselves. At the other extreme are those who are so altruistic that others are of more importance than themselves- they are self-sacrificial.

While we all can be "bad" and "sinful", some are exceptionally so- to the point that we might consider them "evil". What makes them so? I believe it is psychopathology. There is something wrong with these people. It is not that they are possessed, or the devil "makes them do it". It has to do with genetics, neurochemistry, neuroanatomy, trauma and learning.

Psychiatrist, Michael Stone, devised a scale in which he outlines gradations of evil. His scale is somewhat reminiscent of Dante Alighieri's *Inferno* in which Dante describes levels of hell, based in large part on the Seven Deadly Sins known during early Christian times. These sins were Pride, Envy, Greed, Sloth, Lust, Anger, and Gluttony. In the shallowest level of hell were virtuous pagans whose only sin was not knowing Christ (as they lived prior to Christ's birth). Murderers and "usurers" (those who lend money at unreasonably high rates) were both at the same level seven. Even deeper into hell were found seducers, flatterers, hypocrites and thieves. At the lowest level were traitors to country and family.

Michael Stone makes a distinction between impulsive acts of evil such as crimes of passion and those acts that are premeditated. Other important factors in Stone's delineation are whether there is psychopathy and whether there is sadism. Stone delineates 22 categories of evil in six broader categories. These six broad categories are:

1. Killing in self-defense or justified homicide (which Stone said does not indicate evil).

2. Impulsive murders in persons without psychopathic features.

3. Persons with a few or no psychopathic traits; murders of a more severe type.

4. Psychopathic features are marked; murders show malice aforethought.

5. Spree or multiple murders; psychopathy is apparent.

6. Serial killers, torturers, sadists.

So, for Stone, aggression, including murder, is less evil if done impulsively and out of passion than is premeditated acts where there is aforethought. Our legal system also recognizes this distinction. Stone also believes the presence of psychopathy is an important factor in the gradation of evil; these are individuals who are extremely self-centered. I will talk more about this in some detail later in this chapter. Finally, Stone believes the most evil individuals are not only completely self-centered, but also actually enjoy the suffering of others. I agree with Stone on this.

Many DSM-V disorders have to do with morality, i.e. the degree of self-centeredness. For some disorders, this might be a surprise. Let me use the example of alcoholism. Genetics is important to alcoholism; twin studies have demonstrated strong evidence that biology is more important than upbringing in the development of alcoholism. In other words, if you were adopted as an infant, your biological family whom you have never met is the much more relevant factor than the family that raised you in whether or not you are going to develop alcoholism. Neuroanatomy and neurochemistry are also relevant for genetic reasons; in the case of alcoholism the limbic system of the brain and the neurochemical dopamine are important.

So what does morality have to do with alcoholism? "The Big Book" (1976) is the primary text used by Alcoholics Anonymous, arguably the most successful organization in the world for the treatment of alcoholism. The Big Book says that most people can recover from alcoholism, and the one group of people who often don't recover are "men and women who are constitutionally incapable of being honest with themselves."

Selfishness- self-centeredness! That, we think, is the root of our troubles. Driven by a hundred forms of fear, self-delusion, self-seeking, and self-pity, we step on the toes of our fellows and they retaliate. Sometimes they hurt us, seemingly without provocation, but we invariably find that at some time in the past we have made decisions based on self which later placed us in a position to be hurt.

So our troubles, we think, are basically of our own making. They arise out of ourselves, and the alcoholic is an extreme example of self-will run riot, though he usually doesn't think so. Above everything, we alcoholics must be rid of this self-ishness. We must, or it kills us! (Big Book, 1976, p. 62).

Genetics (Nature)

In psychology there has been a long-term debate about whether human behavior is primarily influenced by nature (i.e. genetics) or nurture (i.e. the environment including pre-natal environment). In general, both are important, and the interaction between the two is found to be particularly important. So what about with the construct of morality? When individuals are especially altruistic, empathetic and loving, what causes this to be so? When individuals are par-ticularly self-centered, uncaring, violent and hateful, does this occur because of genes, the way they are raised, or some other factor, such as the influences of a malevolent deity such as Satan? The answer is not with the supernatural; rather, science does give us some answers. We will start by looking at genes.

Traits are often determined by genes. The genome is the complete set of genetic information that an organism has. Human cells have about 25,000 different genes scattered among our 46 chromosomes. Genes are a segment of DNA (deoxyribonucleic acid) that are passed on from generation to generation. All living creatures have genomes that consist of DNA. DNA is the genetic blueprint for creating organ-isms. There is much common genetic material between vari-ous living creatures. For example, humans and fruit flies share approximately 60% of their genes. Humans and chim-panzees share about 99% of their genes. All humans share among each other 99.9% of genetics; we vary from each other only because of that one tenth of one percent of genes.

Many people think of evolution as being *survival of the fittest*, and what we usually think of with this phrase is whether a species survives, changes, or goes extinct. The ethologist, Richard Dawkins, presents a different take on this, however, in his best selling book *The Selfish Gene* (1989). Dawkins maintains that we should think in terms of the survival of the gene rather than survival of a species. It is the gene that is "selfish" in its desire to survive, potentially to immortality. Selfish genes lead to selfish behavior by individuals.

Dawkins writes that atoms tend to link up and form molecules. "If a group of atoms in the presence of energy falls into a stable pattern it will tend to stay that way." Before life began on earth, Dawkins hypothesizes that simple compounds existed which may have included water, carbon dioxide, methane and ammonia (these compounds are known to exist on other planets in our solar system). Dawkins hypothesizes that amino acids developed and then organic substances such as purines and pyrimidines. "These are building blocks of the genetic molecule, DNA itself". Organic substances evolved in the *primeval soup*.

"At some point a particularly remarkable molecule was formed by accident." Dawkins refers to it as the *replicator*. Dawkins hypothesizes that this molecule had the ability to make copies of itself, and as a result "a new kind of 'stability' came into the world." However, inevitably "mistakes" would happen in the copying process. "As mis-copyings were made and propagated, the primeval soup became filled by a population not of identical replicas, but of several varieties of replicating molecules, all 'descended' from the same ancestor." (Dawkins, 1989).

Dawkins goes on to hypothesize that over time the replicators began to construct containers to inhabit in order to increase the chances of survival. These "containers" are organisms, including eventually humans; the replicators are now referred to as *genes*. Humans and other animals live a matter of only decades. DNA, on the other hand, continues for thousands or millions of years, continuing to exist from one "survival machine" (Dawkins' term for the organisms that contain the DNA) to another, to another, etc. Genes are potentially immortal.

All living things on this planet, whether bacteria, carrots, cows, or humans share common genes. Dawkins presents an intriguing perspective that evolution is about the survival and change of genes rather than survival and change of individuals or species. "Individuals are not stable things, they are fleeting. Chromosomes too are shuffled into oblivion, like hands of cards soon after they are dealt. But the cards themselves survive the shuffling. The cards are the genes. The genes are not destroyed by crossing-over, they merely change partners and march on." (Dawkins, 1989).

So within that one-tenth of one percent in which humans vary from each other, what role do genes play in morality? Psychologist Adrian Raine (2013) reviewed studies that investigated the genetic influence on criminality, antisocial behaviors, aggression and violence. Raine reports that studies have been done comparing adopted children on levels of criminality. These studies found that children who had criminal biological fathers were much more likely to become criminals themselves than the adopted children whose fathers were not criminals.

Better studies would be to compare fraternal and identical twins on a construct, in this case crime and aggression. Fraternal twins share 50% of their genes with each other (just as normal siblings do), while identical twins are completely alike genetically. Studies, according to Raine, indicate that identical twins are much more similar in terms of crime and aggression than are fraternal twins.

An even better type of study would be to compare identical twins who are separated at birth. This is a way of separating out genetics from environment. Raine reports that these studies suggest that these twins "are surprisingly similar with respect to antisocial personality" despite being raised in different households. Raine believes that "half of the answer to why some of us are antisocial while others are not is due to genetics."

Raine also reports that aggression and violence are heritable. "A meta-analysis of 103 studies compared heritability of aggressive behavior with rule-breaking, nonaggressive behavior. Nonaggressive antisocial behavior was 48 percent heritable, while aggressive behavior was 65 percent heritable."

Environment (Nurture)

Certainly our early upbringing and home-life has a significant effect on the development of morality, right? Actually Tom Bouchard (2003), behavioral geneticist from the University of Minnesota, and Adrian Raine (2013) in analyzing their own and others' research conclude that parental upbringing has minimal impact on future values and morality. Although our children frequently end up with similar values as our own, they suggest that it is likely genetics rather than upbringing that has the much more significant influence. "Recent twin studies of adults, including twins reared apart, and one adoption study, suggest that social attitudes such as Religiousness, Conservatism, and Authoritarianism are perhaps as heritable as personality traits" (i.e. "close to zero"). Psychologist Steven Pinker also has commented on this:

Consider the fact that children of immigrants end up with the accent, values, and norms of their peers, not of their parents. That tells us that children are socialized in their peer group rather than in their families: it takes a village to raise a child. And studies of adopted children have found that they end up with personalities and IQ scores that are correlated with those of their biological siblings but uncorrelated with those of their adopted siblings. That tells us that adult personality and intelligence are shaped by genes, and also by chance (since the correlations are far from perfect, even among identical twins), but are not shaped by parents, at least not by anything they do with all their children. (Pinker, 2011).

In regards specifically to antisocial behavior, Raine in his own research found that "familial home influences accounted for on average 22 percent of the total variance in antisocial behavior. In contrast, environmental influences outside the family accounted for 33 percent of the variance." (Raine, 2013). The author reports that other studies on antisocial behavior (over 100 of them) also suggest similar results. Raine reports that even by the age of nine peers begin to have significant influence. Other environmental factors that have effects on violence and antisocial behaviors are bullying and exposure to violence, and this includes witnessing violence in the home and in the neighborhood and also exposure to media violence (Sapolsky, 2017).

The famous British psychologist/psychiatrist John Bowlby did extensive research on the effects of institutionalization on children. He found that children who grow up in orphanages frequently show a variety of emotional problems, including the inability to form intimate and lasting relationships with others. He looked into the backgrounds of forty-four juvenile offenders and wrote an analysis in *Forty-Four Juvenile Thieves* (1946). These juveniles had prolonged separations from their mothers in their early lives, and as a result they had what Bowlby termed "affectionless psychopathy". It is believed that there is a critical period for attachment to a primary caregiver from about six-months old to two-years old.

Raine (2013) believes that "maternal rejection" is an important factor for producing violence in people. "First, rearing in a public-care institution in the first year of life was critical. Second, an attempt to abort the fetus also came up trumps. These were the two elements of maternal rejection that interacted with birth complications in producing later violence." Raine said the combination of a poor early home environment with birth complications particularly predispose individuals to adult violence. Birth complications include hypoxia (lack of oxygen for a period of time), preeclampsia, maternal bleeding, and maternal infections causing a reduction in blood supply to the placenta.

In a discussion about environmental factors that affect propensity to violence and other antisocial behaviors, we must include the *prenatal* environment. "We now know that if a mother smokes during pregnancy it not only has negative consequences on brain development, but it also leads to increased rates of conduct disorder and aggression in her offspring." (Raine, 2013) Raine also discusses the relationship of fetal alcohol syndrome to crime and delinquency. Raine referenced a study that "documented that drinking any alcohol at all during pregnancy tripled the odds that the child would have clinically significant delinquency."

Raine also discussed a number of other prenatal insults which affect later antisocial behavior. These issues include poor nutrition and being the victim of famine and prenatal exposure to lead, cadmium, manganese and mercury. Although genetics may play some role, pregnancy disorders are believed to sometimes cause what are known as *minor physical anomalies*. These are physical abnormalities which include cleft palate issues, macrocephaly (abnormally large head), low set ears, a particular pattern of the crease in palms, fissured tongue and other abnormalities which are generally benign in and of themselves. They do indicate, however, congenital irregularities. A 1978 article in *Science* suggested that a brief examination for minor physical anomalies in male newborns could predict later increased levels of peer aggression, impulsivity, and poorer attention in these children at three year old. (Waldrop, *et al.*, 1978)

Robert Sapolsky (2017) has discussed the impact of "childhood adversity" in the development of antisocial behaviors and violence in later adults. "Basically, childhood adversity increases the odds of an adult having (a) depression, anxiety, and/or substance abuse; (b) impaired cognitive capabilities, particularly related to frontocortical function; (c) impaired impulse control and emotion regulation; (d) antisocial behavior, including violence; and (e) relationships that replicate the adversities of childhood (e.g., staying with an abusive partner)." (Sapolsky, 2017).

Anda *et al* (2006) examined correlations between adverse childhood experiences and a number of negative outcomes.

The sample consisted of 17,337 adult HMO members. Eight categories of adverse childhood experiences (ACE) were derived from the questionnaire: emotional, physical and sexual abuse, household dysfunction, substance abuse, mental illness, mother treated violently, incarcerated household member, and parental separation or divorce. Of the sample group, 36% had none of the above adverse childhood experiences, 26% had one, 15% had two, 9% had three, and 12% had four or more of the ACE. The results showed a strong correlation between the number of ACE and psychiatric illness (depression, anxiety, panic, and hallucinations), and several other issues including obesity, somatic complaints, smoking, injected drugs, promiscuity, sexual dissatisfaction, anger, and partner violence.

Robert Sapolsky (2017) also writes about the harmful sequelae of childhood adversity. Chronic early life stressors affect the H-P-A axis (hypothalamic-pituitary-adrenal) which causes excessive glucocorticoid levels which damage the brain. There is evidence for decreased volume in the hippocampus, an important brain structure for memory. These effects on the hippocampus also affect the production of BDNF (brain-derived neurotrophic factor) which likely contributes to impaired maturation and functioning of the frontal cortex. There is also evidence, according to Sapolsky, that childhood adversity can have affects on another brain structure, the amygdala, but this time increasing the size of the structure rather than atrophying it. The amygdala is important for impulse control. "Normally, around adolescence the frontal cortex gains the ability to inhibit the amygdala, saying, 'I wouldn't do this if I were you.' But after childhood adversity, the amygdala develops the ability to inhibit the frontal cortex, saying, 'I'm doing this and just try to stop me.'" (Sapolsky, 2017).

Neuroanatomy

One of the most important brain structures in regards to the topic of morality, violence and antisocial behaviors is the frontal cortex. It is the last part of the brain to fully develop; in fact, it is not fully developed until the mid-20s. It is responsible for what is called *executive functioning*. This includes the ability to focus and concentrate, to be able to initiate tasks without prompting, the ability to filter out irrelevant information, to not be distractible, planning and organizational abilities, reasoning, and the ability to self-monitor and self-control. Individuals with deficits in the frontal lobes are often impulsive, erratic in behaviors, are emotionally labile or have flattened affect, and can be rigid in thinking. The impulsivity, lack of planning and poor judgment seen in adolescence is a consequence of not fully developed frontal lobes. The frontal lobes are also important for the development of empathy, sympathy and moral reasoning. Many of the above symptoms described above are also seen with ADHD, a disorder associated with frontal lobe deficits.

A famous clinical case of a person with frontal lobe damage was Phineas Gage, a foreman of a railroad construction crew. Gage was an amiable, respected, and responsible man. On September 13, 1848 he had a very serious accident in which an accidental gunpowder explosion blew a 13 lb. iron tamping rod through his skull. It entered through the left side of his face and exited out the top-front of his skull and landed eighty feet away covered with parts of his left frontal cortex. Amazingly after a couple of minutes his body began to move, and he began to groan; he was still alive!. He was brought to a doctor, and amazingly he survived and got better. However, friends and acquaintances reported he was "no longer Gage". This responsible and balanced man became impulsive, irresponsible, promiscuous, and a drunkard. He was fired from a job due to his being unreliable. Gage did not lose language, motor functioning or intellectual abilities in its normal sense; the thing that changed was his personality and moral character.

Damage to the prefrontal cortex "give rise to disinhibited anger after minimal provocation, characterized by an individual showing little regard for the consequences of affect and behavior." There is an amazingly high proportion of violent offenders who have had a history of trauma to the frontal cortex (Sapolsky, 2017), (Cherkasky,& Hollander, 2005). Tumors to the frontal lobes are also associated with behavioral and personality changes. "The orbitofrontal syndrome is characterized by changes in personality. These patients typically present with irritability and lability. Cognitively, patients with this syndrome often demonstrate poor judgment and a lack of insight into their behavior. These patients have sometimes been referred to as *pseudopsychopathic.* (Price, Goetz & Lovell, 2005).

There are progressive dementias that also affect the frontal lobe. Unlike Alzheimer's Disease where the earliest manifestation is generally deficits in memory for recent events, individuals with frontotemporal dementias (FTD) may not have any deficits with recent memory. They often do have changes in personality; they may become apathetic, or they may become disinhibited. "Disinhibited patients are often boisterous and prone to make vulgar or socially inappropriate remarks, to exhibit undue familiarity with strangers, and to have poor judgment, and they may be unusually irritable." (White & Cummings, 2005). A common sequellae of FTD is also hypersexuality (Mendez & Shapira, 2013) and "sociopathic" behaviors such physical assaults and unsolicited sexual acts. "On interview, the FTD patients with sociopathic acts were aware of their behavior and knew that it was wrong but could not prevent themselves from acting impulsively. They claimed subsequent remorse, but they did not act on it or show concern for the consequences." (Mendez et al, 2005).

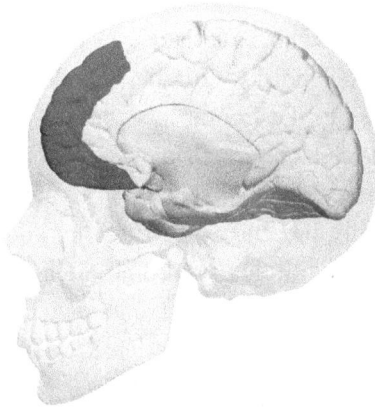

Pre-frontal Cortex
(Courtesy of Wikimedia)

Another important brain structure for violence and morality is the amygdala. This is a bilateral structure which is part of the limbic system (which is very important for emotional functioning). There is evidence to support a dysfunctional limbic system in psychopaths (and others with impaired moral functioning). Raine (2013) reported research that suggests an 18 percent reduction in the volume of the amygdala in psychopaths, particularly in the central, basolateral and cortical nuclei. By implanting an electrode into the amygdala and stimulating it, one can induce a rage response. During the 1970s highly controversial surgeries were done on individuals to control severe aggression; i.e. amygdalas were removed (amygdalotomies).

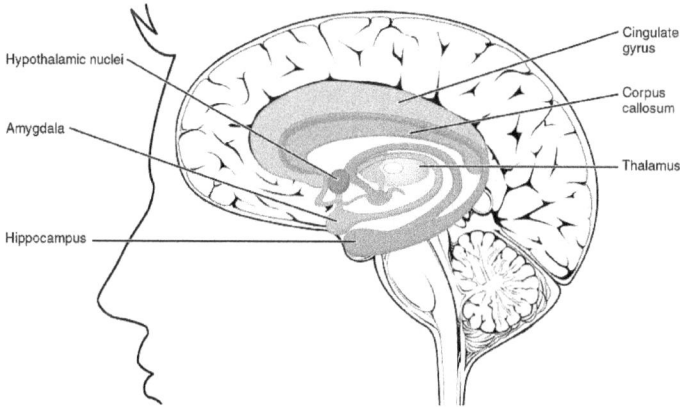

(courtesy of Wikipedia)

Other brain structures have been implicated in violence and psychopathy as well: The hippocampus is a brain structure particularly important for memory. There has been some research to support impaired functioning in violent offenders and psychopaths (Soderstrom, H. et al, 2000) (Kiehl, K., 2006) (Muller, J. et al, 2003) (Amen, Hanks & Green, 2007)

The cingulate cortex also appears to be a pertinent structure. The anterior portion is important for the experience of empathy, and the posterior portion has been implicated in psychopathy and aggression. A larger and superior functioning corpus collosum has been found in psychopaths. The angular gyrus has also been implicated in violent offenders (lower glucose metabolism and reduced cerebral blood flow). (Raine, 2013).

Psychologist Simon Baron-Cohen (2011) delineated a number of brain structures important for empathy: the medial prefrontal cortex, the orbito-frontal cortex, the frontal operculum, the inferior frontal gyrus, the caudal anterior cingulate cortex, the middle cingulate cortex, the anterior insula, the temporoparietal junction, the posterior superior temporal sulcus, the somatosensory cortex, the inferior parietal lobule, and the amygdala.

Neurotransmitters and Hormones

The various brain structures mentioned in the above section of this chapter are made up of neurons, specialized cells of the brain. Neurons communicate with each other via chemicals called neurotransmitters. These neurotransmitters are also an important topic when discussing morality and violence. One important neurotransmitter is *serotonin*. Low levels of serotonin in the brain are associated with heightened levels of aggression. This is seen in both humans and other animals. It is not associated with premeditated, well thought out aggression but rather with impulsive violence. For example, this would include a spouse who catches their lover having an affair and responds with rage and an aggressive act that they would not have done if they had the time to ponder their response.

DSM-5 is the latest version of the American Psychiatric Association's manual of mental health disorders. One disorder listed in it is *Intermittent Explosive Disorder*. The essential feature of this disorder is brief unexpected verbal or physical aggressive outbursts that are in response to minor provocations. The outbursts are usually impulsive and anger-based. One of the most common treatments for this is prescriptions for SSRIs (Selective Serotonin Reuptake Inhibitors) which are medications which by blocking the re-absorption of serotonin makes more serotonin available to affect other neurons.

Another important neurotransmitter is *dopamine*. When individuals are brought into psychiatric hospitals against their wills and are combative and agitated, more than likely they will be given an injection of haloperidol (or a similar drug). These antipsychotic medications (or *neuroleptics*) have as a mechanism of action the blockade of D2 dopamine receptors. "The introduction of neuroleptics in the 1950s fundamentally changed how clinicians managed aggression in psychotics, depressives, schizophrenics, mentally retarded, nonpsychotic character disordered delinquents, amphetamine abusers, alcoholics, or patients suffering from organic brain syndrome" (Miczek & Fish, 2006).

Schizophrenia is a chronic disease which is characterized by what are known as "positive symptoms" (hallucinations, delusions, hostility, agitation, disorganized speech and behaviors, ideas of reference, illogical thought process) and "negative symptoms" (anhedonia, poor social skills, poor personal hygiene, blunted affect, emotional and social with-drawal, difficulty in abstract thinking). Although most indi-viduals with schizophrenia are not violent, there is an increased incidence of aggression and violence in schizo-phrenic individuals than there is in the general population. Medications that block dopamine in certain pathways are helpful for decreasing hostility and violent behaviors.

Newer "second generation" antipsychotic medications have for the most part replaced the older neuroleptic drugs, and they have the additional advantage of blocking serotonin 2A receptors, which is helpful for the amelioration of negative symptoms of schizophrenia as well as the positive symptoms.

Glutamate and GABA are also relevant neurotransmitters. Glutamate is the major excitatory neurotransmitter in the brain and GABA is the major inhibitory NT. Glutamate excites neural circuits and limbic regions such as the amygdala increasing the possibility of an inappropriate response to threatening stimuli. GABA, on the other hand, inhibits aggressive behaviors. (Miczek & Fish, 2006). Medications which increase GABA and/or decrease Glutamate are effective for decreasing aggression. This would include patients with *bipolar* disorder. Látalová (2009) in her review of research on bipolar disorder and aggression reports that "the prevalence of aggressive behavior after age 15 years was 0.66% in persons without lifetime psychiatric disorder, but 25.34% in bipolar 1 disorder".

I'll make mention of two other neurotransmitters: *Oxytocin and Vasopressin.* Oxytocin in particular is important for social bonding, maternal bonding with infants, and empathy. "Infuse oxytocin into the brain of a virgin rat, and she'll act maternally- retrieving, grooming, and licking pups. Block the actions of oxytocin in a rodent mother, and she'll stop maternal behaviors, including nursing." (Sapolsky, 2017).

Borderline Personality Disorder

I have mentioned some psychiatric disorders above that have moral implications, i.e. correlations with increased violence and aggression and decreased empathy. The Diagnostic and Statistical Manual of Mental Disorders-5 (2013) , the latest version of the diagnostic manual of the American Psychiatric Association, describes not only "clinical issues" that are the usual focus for psychiatric/psychological treatment, but also *personality disorders*. DSM-5 lists ten specific personality disorders and defines personality disorders in general as "an enduring pattern of inner experience and behavior that deviates markedly from the expectations of the individual's culture, is pervasive and inflexible, has an onset in adolescence or early adulthood, is stable over time, and leads to distress or impairment." I would like to now discuss three particularly personality disorders that I believe are relevant to the topic of morality. The first P.D. I will discuss is Borderline Personality Disorder.

Borderline PD is defined in DSM-5 as "a pervasive pattern of instability of interpersonal relationships, self-image, and affects, and marked impulsivity". To be diagnosed with BPD, one also needs to meet five or more of nine specific criteria in the DSM-5. Borderlines typically have difficult and traumatic childhoods; it is not uncommon for them to be victims of abuse of various kinds. Borderlines commonly self-refer for counseling as they often feel significant psychological distress. They have difficulties in interpersonal relationships; they are prone to feelings of abandonment while simultaneously being very uncomfortable with emotional intimacy. A book written on BPD by Kreisman and Straus was aptly entitled "I Hate You-Don't Leave Me". In addition, they have significant difficulties with emotional regulation.

The reason I am including this group of individuals in a discussion of morality is due to their significant deficits with empathy. Borderlines often describe themselves as feeling "empty" inside. They struggle with self-identity; they don't have a sense of self. They don't know deep down who they really are. If one does not know who one is, how can one be able to figure out who others are? These individuals have trouble reading the emotions of others, and they also have difficulties responding to others in an emotionally appropriate way. Borderlines are typically very self-centered, which is for me a hallmark of immorality. Referring back to my bell curve earlier in this chapter outlining the continuum of morality, I define immorality as being primarily extreme self-centeredness and lack of concern about others.

Why do borderlines lack empathy, one of the most important ingredients for morality? Psychologist Simon Baron-Cohen (2011) shares the hypothesis that early childhood abuse and neglect changes the physiology and functioning of the brain. "There is decreased binding of neurotransmitters to one of the serotonin receptors. Just as we might expect, these abnormalities occur in brain regions within the empathy circuit." (Cohen, 2011). These brain regions include, according to Cohen, the ventromedial prefrontal cortex, the middle cingulate cortex, areas of the temporal lobe, the orbital frontal cortex, the amygdala, the inferior frontal gyrus, and the superior temporal sulcus.

Narcissistic Personality Disorder

Narcissistic PD is defined by DSM-5 as "a pervasive pattern of grandiosity (in fantasy or behavior), need for admiration, and lack of empathy, beginning by early adulthood and present in a variety of contexts". One needs to meet criteria for five or more of nine specific listed criteria in the DSM-5. Narcissists are concerned only about themselves. They have a sense of entitlement; they think they are deserving of special treatment, not warranted by any actual accomplishments. Because they don't care about others, they are exploitative. They will use others to get what they want; others are a means to their own individual ends. And so they are immoral in that they are pervasively self-centered; they do not have concern about the needs of others. Baron-Cohen (2011) said there have not been studies done on the neural circuitry of the brains of narcissists.

Psychopathy

Unlike Borderline PD and Narcissistic PD, *Psychopathy* is not a diagnosis in the DSM-5. There are related diagnoses, however: Antisocial Personality Disorder and Conduct Disorder. In addition, there are two other terms that are similar to psychopathy, i.e. sociopathy and malignant narcissism. I will start out by delineating the differences between these terms. Let us start out with the DSM-5 diagnosis of Antisocial Personality Disorder. It is defined in DSM-5 as "a pervasive pattern of disregard for and violation of the rights of others, occurring since age 15". To qualify for the diagnosis, three (or more) of the following must be present:

1. Failure to conform to social norms with respect to lawful behaviors, as indicated by repeatedly performing acts that are grounds for arrest.

2. Deceitfulness, as indicated by repeated lying, use of aliases, or conning others for personal profit or pleasure.

3. Impulsivity or failure to plan ahead.

4. Irritability and aggressiveness, as indicated by repeated physical fights or assaults.

5. Reckless disregard for safety of self or others.

6. Consistent irresponsibility, as indicated by repeated failure to sustain consistent work behavior or honor financial obligations.

7. Lack of remorse, as indicated by being indifferent to or rationalizing having hurt, mistreated, or stolen from another.

A related diagnosis in DSM-5 is Conduct Disorder, defined as "a repetitive and persistent pattern of behavior in which the basic rights of others or major age-appropriate societal norms or rules are violated, as manifested by the presence of at least three of the following 15 criteria in the past 12 months from any of the categories below, with at least one criterion present in the past 6 months:

Aggression to People and Animals

1. Often bullies, threatens, or intimidates others.

2. Often initiates physical fights.

3. Has used a weapon that can cause serious physical harm to others (e.g., a bat, brick, broken bottle, knife, gun).

4. Has been physically cruel to people.

5. Has been physically cruel to animals.

6. Has stolen while confronting a victim (e.g., mugging, purse snatching, extortion, armed robbery).

7. Has forced someone into sexual activity.

Destruction of Property

8. Has deliberately engaged in fire setting with the intention of causing serious damage.

9. Has deliberately destroyed others' property (other than by fire setting).

Deceitfulness or Theft

10. Has broken into someone else's house, building, or car.

11. Often lies to obtain goods or favors or to avoid obligations (i.e., "cons" others).

12. Has stolen items of nontrivial value without confronting a victim (e.g., shoplifting, but without breaking and entering; forgery).

Serious Violations of Rules

13. Often stays out at night despite parental prohibitions, beginning before age 13 years.

14. Has run away from home overnight at least twice while living in the parental or parental surrogate home, or once without returning for a lengthy period.

15. Is often truant from school, beginning before age 13 years.

There are three possible subtypes of Conduct Disorder: Childhood-onset type where individuals show some symptomatology prior to the age of ten, Adolescent-onset type where individuals show no symptomatology prior to the age of ten, and unspecified onset where there is insufficient information to determine when the first symptoms began. If the individual is 18 years old or older and they meet criteria for Antisocial Personality Disorder, the clinician would use that diagnosis and not Conduct Disorder. In other words, an Antisocial PD Diagnosis would subsume a diagnosis of Conduct Disorder.

DSM-5 estimates the prevalence of Antisocial PD in the general population as being between 2% and 3.3%, although in other populations (e.g. prison populations and substance abuse populations) the prevalence might be as high as over 70%. Antisocial PD is much more prevalent than is psychopathy. "APD is three or four times more common than psychopathy in the general population and in prisons." "Psychopaths make up about 15 percent of the prison population." (Babiak & Hare, 2006).

A diagnosis of APD is based primarily on an assessment of behaviors, whereas psychopathy might be best thought of as a disorder of personality. Hare (1993) opines that personality traits such as empathy and egocentricity are considered too difficult for the average clinician to assess, and so a diagnosis of APD was based upon behaviors which can be more objectively assessed.

The DSM is a manual that focuses only on the diagnosis of mental disorders. ICD, on the other hand, is a classification system for all diseases, including mental health issues. ICD stands for International Classification of Diseases, and currently it is in the tenth edition. There is a diagnosis in this classification system that is closer to psychopathy than is APD in the DSM. It is called *Dyssocial Personality Disorder*. The following are the criteria for this disorder:

1. Callous unconcern for the feelings of others and lack of the capacity for empathy.

2. Gross and persistent attitude of irresponsibility and disregard for social norms, rules, and obligations.

3. Incapacity to maintain enduring relationships.

4. Very low tolerance to frustration and a low threshold for discharge of aggression, including violence.

5. Incapacity to experience guilt and to profit from experience, particularly punishment.

6. Marked proneness to blame others or to offer plausible rationalizations for the behavior bringing the subject into conflict with society.

7.   Persistent irritability.

The most well known researchers of psychopathy are Hervey Cleckley who wrote *The Mask of Sanity* (1982) and Robert Hare who authored *Without Conscience: The Disturbing World of the Psychopaths Among Us* and who coauthored with Paul Babiak *Snakes in Suits: When Psychopaths Go To Work.* Cleckley uses the following adjectives to describe psychopaths: "arrogant, shameless, immoral, impulsive, antisocial, superficial, alert, self-assured, boastful, callous, remorseless, charming, irresponsible." Babiak and Hare (2006) report that "psychopaths are without conscience and incapable of empathy, guilt, or loyalty to anyone but themselves."

The term "psychopath" is somewhat unfortunate in that it is very close to the term "psychopathology", a term with very different meaning. Psychopathology is a broad term that refers to the study of all mental illnesses and psychological impairments. Psychopathy, on the other hand, is just one disorder among all psychological disorders.

There also is confusion between the terms "psychopath" and "*sociopath*". The two terms are frequently used interchange-ably. However, Babiak and Hare (2006) explain that sociopathy refers to attitudes and behaviors that are consid-ered normal within a subculture but are considered antisocial and abnormal by the larger society. An example might be with a gang. There was a television show about a motorcy-cle gang known as the Sons of Anarchy (this was both the name of the motorcycle club and the television show). This club was a good example of sociopaths. The members of the club followed norms that most in the larger society would consider immoral and antisocial. Many criminals could be considered sociopaths. Psychopathy is more rare.

Another term is "*malignant narcissism*". I believe the term was first coined by psychologist Erich Fromm in 1964. He described it as the "quintessence of evil". The term has also been used by the psychoanalyst Otto Kernberg. To my understanding, malignant narcissism and psychopathy are essentially the same, although the former may include sadism, which is the enjoyment of seeing others suffer.

Psychopathy is most frequently diagnosed using a tool developed by Robert Hare called the Hare Psychopathy Checklist, currently in the 2nd revised edition (PCL-R). The following are the items to be assessed from the PCL-R:

1. Glibness/Superficial Charm
2. Grandiose Sense of Self Worth
3. Need for Stimulation/Proneness to Boredom
4. Pathological Lying
5. Conning/Manipulative
6. Lack of Remorse or Guilt
7. Shallow Affect
8. Callous/Lack of Empathy
9. Parasitic Lifestyle
10. Poor Behavioral Controls
11. Promiscuous Sexual Behavior
12. Early Behavioral Problems
13. Lack of Realistic, Long-Term Goals
14. Impulsivity
15. Irresponsibility
16. Failure to Accept Responsibility for Own Actions
17. Many Short-Term Marital Relationships
18. Juvenile Delinquency
19. Revocation of Conditional Release
20. Criminal Versatility

In scoring the PCL-R, two points are given to an item if it is "a reasonably good match in most essential respects", one point if it partly applies or if there is some uncertainty, and no points if the item does not apply. So, as there are 20 items, there is potential to get 40 points on the measure. According to Babiak and Hare (2006) "Most people in the general population would score less than 5 on the PCL-R, whereas the average score for male and female criminals is about 22 and 19 respectively. A cut score of 30 typically is used to identify psychopaths." "About 15 percent of male offenders and about 10 percent of female offenders obtain a score of at least 30."

It is estimated that 15 to 20 percent of criminals are psychopaths, but "psychopaths are responsible for more than 50 percent of the serious crimes committed" (Hare, 1993). Hare believes "perhaps half of the repeat or serial rapists are psychopaths. Their acts are the result of a potent mixture: uninhibited expression of sexual drives and fantasies, desire for power and control, and perception of the victims as objects of pleasure or satisfaction." Not all psychopaths are criminals; there are many individuals who are successful in sales, business, politics, and other endeavors who are psychopaths. The critical personality characteristics are lack of conscience, lack of guilt, lack of empathy, and extremely self-centeredness.

I agree with Erich Fromm that malignant narcissism and psychopathy are "quintessential evil". On my morality bell curve, these individuals would be at the far end. Evil is about character. So what makes a person a psychopath? Or put another way, what makes someone evil? It does not have to do with supernaturalism.

Many people believe that "a bad seed" is the result of poor parenting. Many would like to believe that if we raise our children to be moral and/or to love and fear God they will end up as good kids and later good adults. Unfortunately, there is a lack of evidence that good parenting and upbringing will prevent the development of psychopathy. R.J.R. Blair is a well known researcher in this area. He said "Currently, there are no known environmental factors (including trauma and neglect) that can give rise to the pathophysiology seen in psychopathy." (Blair, 2008).

There is evidence the genes and heredity do play a role, however. In a 2006 research study of 1,090 monozygotic and dizygotic twin pairs aged 16-17, Larsson, Andershed and Lichtenstein (2006) concluded that their results showed a strong genetic influence on one having a "psychopathic personality", and in particular they cited strong genetic influence on the sub-factors of being callous/unemotional and on being impulsive/irresponsible.

There is evidence for differences in the brains of psychopaths from that of normal controls. The frontal lobes have particularly been implicated (Raine, 2013) (Sapolsky, 2017) (Hare, 1993) (Baron-Cohen, 2011) (Koenigs, 2012) (Blair, 2008). The amygdala is another structure very important in psychopathy (Raine, 2013) (Blair, 2008) Sapolsky, 2017) (Baron-Cohen, 2011). There also are differences with the autonomic nervous system (Raine, 2013) (Scarpa and Raine, 2006). Also implicated are structural deficits of the hippocampus, corpus callosum, and striatum. "These structural abnormalities are likely not the result of some discrete disease process or obvious trauma. Such causes would if anything result in overall volume reductions to these structures. Our findings are much more complex than that. The right hippocampus is *larger* than the left in psychopaths. The striatum is *larger.* The corpus callosum also has a *bigger* volume. And the corpus callosum is not only *longer* in psychopaths than in controls, it's also *thinner.* So what's the explanation here? It is likely that this shape distortion is neurodevelopmental in nature." (Raine, 2013).

Robert Hare wrote that his belief was that psychopathy develops as the result of a combination of biological and social factors. "In effect, the elements needed for the development of psychopathy- including a profound inability to experience empathy and the complete range of emotions, including fear- are provided in part by nature and possibly by some unknown biological influences on the developing fetus and neonate. As a result, the capacity for developing internal controls and conscience and for making emotional 'connections' with others is greatly reduced." (Hare, 1993). Hare goes on to say that this biological endowment does not pre-destine one's outcome; environmental factors also have some effects, either ameliorating or exacerbating.

Another important distinction to make is between cognitive empathy and emotional empathy. Many of the readers might be aware that a major deficit for individuals in the autism spectrum is lack of empathy. Does this mean they don't care about others? No, that does not appear to be a deficit at all. Baron-Cohen (2011) said individuals with autism are "the mirror image" of psychopaths. "Psychopaths have intact cognitive empathy but reduced affective empathy, while people with Asperger Syndrome, a form of autism, have intact affective empathy but reduced cognitive empathy. The result is that people with Asperger Syndrome do care about others, while struggling to 'read' them." Psychopaths "don't care about others, while at the same time 'read' them with ease."

(Baron-Cohen, 2011). Shamey-Tsoory, Aharon-Peretz and Perry (2009) write that the inferior frontal gyrus is important for emotional empathy, while the ventromedial prefrontal cortex is important for cognitive empathy.

In summary, genetics and biology appear to be the preponderant factor for the most extreme manifestation of evil, the psychopath. Such individuals certainly have been responsible for much suffering in the world. For example, Steven Pinker (2011) has written that most historians conclude that without the single individual, Adolf Hitler, there would not have been a Holocaust. However, I believe that most of the problems and suffering in the world has been the result of individuals more toward the middle of the bell curve and not at the very extreme. It is the *average* immorality, sinfulness, selfishness (however you want to put it) that is of most concern to me. That is the topic of the next chapter.

Chapter 3

Sin as Deficits in

Moral Development

In chapter two of this book I presented information on individuals at the far end of one side of the bell curve, the side of evil; the psychopath. I would like to start out this chapter by briefly sharing information about an individual at the other far end of the bell curve; the side of goodness and selflessness. I believe an excellent example is Mother Teresa. Agnes Gonzha Bojaxhiu was born in August of 1910 to an Albanian Catholic family. When Agnes was 12 she felt a calling to religious service. Six years later she decided to join the Loreto Sisters of Dublin and to become a nun. Agnes completed her postulancy in Dublin, and on December 1, 1928 she boarded a boat for India to begin her missionary service. In May of 1931 she took her first profession of vows and became a full member of the Sisters of Loreto. From then on she took the name of "Teresa". Sister Teresa then moved to Calcutta to begin a teaching career. In 1937 she took her final vows as a nun, and it was at this time she became known as "Mother Teresa".

In 1943 a horrible famine swept through the region, and millions died. Then in 1946, Mother Teresa happened to go out into the city of Calcutta which coincidentally was a day in which great riots broke out between Hindus and Muslims. Four thousand people were killed, and over 100,000 were left homeless. A month later while on a retreat, Mother Teresa had a second calling from God; she felt called to leave her teaching job and to go into the Calcutta slums to work with the poorest of the poor. She obtained nursing training and moved in with the *Dalits*, known as "untouchables". They were at the lowest wrung of Indian society and were unbelievably poor. Mother Teresa not only ministered to them but lived with them. She began a religious community in Calcutta known as the Missionaries of Charity. They established orphanages, medical clinics, soup kitchens, and homes for people with chronic conditions such as AIDS and leprosy. She continued her work there until her death in 1997 at the age of 87.

After devoting a chapter in this book to the subject of evil, I am writing about the life of Mother Teresa to demonstrate a life at the other end of the continuum of morality. It also provides a segue into the topics of sex and gender. Do men and women differ in terms of morality?

"Demonic Males"

I am not aware of differences between men and women in regards to degree of selfishness and self-centeredness, but there does appear to be differences in regards to the specific topic of violence. Richard Wrangham and Dale Peterson (1997) entitled a book coauthored by them as *Demonic Males*. A major point they make in the book is that males by far commit the majority of violent and non-violent crimes. They report that in the United States:

- Man is 9 times more likely than woman to commit murder.

- Man is 78 times more likely to commit forcible rape.

- Man is 10 times more likely to commit armed robbery.

- Man is 6.5 times more likely to commit aggravated assault.

- Man is 8 times more likely to commit violent crime generally.

- Man is 13.5 times more likely to commit fraud.

- Man is 13 times more likely to be arrested for weapons.

- Man is 10 times more likely to burgle.

- Man is 9 times more likely to steal a car.

- Man is 8.5 times more likely to be arrested for drunkenness.

- Man is 8 times more likely to vandalize.

- Man is 7.5 times more likely to fence stolen property.

- Man is 7 times more likely to commit arson.

- Man is 6.5 times more likely to be stopped for drunk driving.

- Man is over 2 times more likely to commit larceny.

- Man is .5 times more likely to commit embezzlement.

Wrangham and Peterson report that women commit more crime than men in only two categories: prostitution and running away from home as teenagers. "Crime statistics from Australia, Botswana, Brazil, Canada, Denmark, England and Wales, Germany, Iceland, India, Kenya, Mexico, Nigeria, Scotland, Uganda, a dozen different locations in the United

States, and Zaire, as well as from thirteenth- and fourteenth-century England and nineteenth-century America- from hunter-gatherer communities, tribal societies, and medieval and modern nation-states- all uncover the same fundamental pattern." (Wrangham and Peterson, 1997).

So why are males more prone to criminality and aggression than females? Many put the blame on testosterone, the primary male *hormone*. In the last chapter I discussed neurotransmitters. The difference between hormones and neurotransmitters is that NTs are chemicals released from one neuron that have effects on other nearby neurons, whereas hormones are chemicals produced by glands that travel through the bloodstream to affect distant organs. Sapolsky (2017) reports "testosterone is far less relevant to aggression than usually assumed."

Testosterone is very important, however, particularly to two critical periods: prenatal development and adolescence. There has been a lot of controversy about sexual orientation (the sex we are attracted to) and gender identity (the gender we feel we are regardless of physical characteristics). However, there is not ambiguity about the sex one is, right? Males have the genotype of XY and a penis, and females have a genotype of XX and a vagina. Well, what about individuals who are XY and have a vagina, or individuals who are XX and have a penis? Things are more complicated than most would think.

Let me first define a couple terms. The term *sex* refers to one's biology, while the term *gender* refers to psychological traits and is heavily influenced by culture. Genotype refers to the specific genes that one has, while phenotype refers to how those genes are expressed. So males would typically have the genotype of XY which would cause a phenotype which includes having testes and a penis. Many people now are having genetic testing done with such companies as "23 And Me". The genetic testing gives us information about the likelihood of having various traits. It also can give us susceptibilities to various medical problems.

How does one become a male or a female? Embryos develop two different ducts: Müllerian ducts and Wolffian ducts. No matter what the genotype of the embryo, both duct systems develop. Müllerian ducts are the precursor to the female reproductive tract, and the Wolffian ducts are the precursor to the male reproductive tract. Testosterone is important in the developing fetus at about three months in terms of whether the fetus becomes male or female. The presence of testosterone causes the Wolffian ducts to develop into the male reproductive system and the Müllerian ducts to degenerate. The absence of testosterone has the opposite effects, i.e. the Müllerian ducts to develop into the female reproductive system and the Wolffian ducts to degenerate. There is a gene on the Y Chromosome (called SRY) that cause sexual development to follow the male pathway.

However, in nature things don't always go the way they are supposed to go. One abnormality is *Androgen Insensitivity Syndrome*. These are XY individuals (i.e. genetic males) who as embryos fail to respond to the presence of testosterone. Consequently as adults they appear completely female (i.e. vagina and breast development) and identify as women. However, they are infertile. Are these individuals male, as they are genetically XY? Or are they female, as they have vaginas and breasts?

Another abnormality is *Congenital Adrenal Hyperplasia*. For these individuals during fetal development there are abnormal amounts of testosterone causing XX fetuses (i.e.

genetic females) to be masculinized and the clitoris to develop into a penis. These individuals are usually raised as girls, although occasionally the more masculinized children are raised as boys.

Some children are born with ambiguous genitalia, with the cause being unknown. It used to be thought that this problem was best rectified by immediate surgery to "normalize" genitalia. Usually the intention of the surgery was to make the genitalia female as this was the easiest remedy. It was thought that the child then would be raised and socialized as a female, and then there would be no further problem. However, this was not the case. Many of these children felt that their gender identity did not correspond to their sex. Although these children's bodies were changed to correspond to a particular gender, their brains were not. Prenatal hormones affect not only the development of genitalia and secondary sexual characteristics (such as whether one develops breasts), but also affects the brain. There are differences in the *brains* of males and females.

There also is a condition called *hermaphroditism*. These children also have some ambiguity in their external genitalia, but the difference between these individuals and the individuals in the previous paragraph is that they also have internal sex organs of both sexes, i.e. ovarian and testicular tissue.

Again, genetic females are XX and males are XY, but occasionally there are anomalies. For example, there is a syndrome called *Klinefelter Syndrome* in which the baby possesses an extra X chromosome or two (i.e. XXY or XXXY). The prevalence of this condition is about 1 in 1000 births. Men with this condition may have low testosterone levels, smaller penis and testicles, sparse body and facial hair, and may have some breast development. They may be infertile, and there is some evidence to suggest there is greater incidence of homosexuality.

Another genetic anomaly is *Turner Syndrome*. These are girls who lack one of the X chromosomes (i.e. XO rather than XX). Prevalence is 1 in 4000 births. These girls tend to be short with a broad neck and chest, and they are infertile. Another genetic syndrome affecting girls is *Triple-X Syndrome* (XXX). Prevalence is 1 in 2000 births. Many of these girls go undiagnosed; there may be mild cognitive deficits and lower fertility.

Yet another genetic anomaly is *XYY Syndrome*. These are males with an extra Y chromosome. Prevalence is 1 in 1500 babies. There is some controversial research to suggest the possibility of increased criminality among such individuals, particularly with sexual offenses.

So testosterone is extremely important during fetal development. Testosterone once again becomes important during adolescence for males. This is the period of time when testosterone levels are the highest; it is also the time period for males when aggression is most prevalent. So does testosterone cause aggression? It does not appear to be so. First of all, there is no correlation between levels of testosterone and aggression in individuals, although abuse of testosterone-like drugs (anabolic steroids) can cause increased aggression. This has been nicknamed "roid rage". In studies where volunteers are administered testosterone, there is no associated increase in aggression.

Robert Sapolsky (2017) has written quite extensively about the effects of testosterone. He notes that being involved in acts of aggression increases levels of testosterone. He also notes that "success in everything from athletics to chess to the stock market boosts testosterone levels." So there is a chicken-egg problem here: does testosterone increase aggression, aggression increase testosterone, or both?

Sapolsky also notes that in some states "chemical castration" is done which inhibits testosterone production or blocks testosterone receptors. Although it appears to be helpful for sex offenders "with intense, obsessive, and pathological urges", it does not appear to be effective for "hostile rapists and those who commit sex crimes motivated by power or anger".

Sapolsky summarizes that testosterone is a small factor to the problem of aggression. The big problem, he says is social learning. "In our world riddled with male violence, the problem isn't that testosterone can increase levels of aggression. The problem is the frequency with which we reward aggression."

Stages of Moral Development

A familiar name in introductory psychology textbooks is that of developmental psychologist Lawrence Kohlberg. His research led to the development of his theory of stages of moral development. Kohlberg (1971) said "For twelve years, I have been studying the development of moral judgment and character primarily by following the same group of 75 boys at three-year intervals from early adolescence (at the beginning the boys were 10 to 16 years of age) through young manhood (they are now 22 to 28 years of age). This study has been supplemented by a series of studies of development in other cultures, and by a set of experimental studies". One of the criticisms of Kohlberg's research was that he only used male subjects.

Kohlberg presented to his subjects a short vignette followed by questioning to determine their level of moral reasoning. The following vignette was used:

In Europe, a woman was near death from a very bad disease, a special kind of cancer. There was one drug that the doctors thought might save her. It was a form of radium that a druggist was charging ten times what the drug cost him to make. He paid $2000 for the radium and charged $2,000 for a small dose of the drug. The sick woman's husband, Heinz, went to everyone he knew to borrow the money, but he could only get together about $1,000 which is half of what it cost. He told the druggist that his wife was dying, and asked him to sell it cheaper or let him pay later. But the druggist said, 'No, I discovered the drug and I'm going to make money from it.' So Heinz got desperate and broke into the man's store to steal the drug for his wife.

Should the husband have done that? Why?

Kohlberg's stages of moral development have some parallels with Jean Piaget's stages of cognitive development. Piaget researched the cognitive development of humans from infancy to adulthood, and he outlined a sequence that he believed was universal no matter what culture a person grew up in. Just as there are physical abilities we expect of children at certain ages (e.g. crawling around nine months, walking around twelve months, etc.), so there are cognitive abilities that we expect at certain ages. For example, at one to one and a half months infants learn to control and coordinate reflexes. At six months the infant can babble and imitate sounds. At nine months the infant can discriminate between parents and other people. Cognitive abilities continue to increase into adolescence and adulthood when some individuals are able to develop reasoning abilities.

Likewise, Kohlberg believed there were invariant sequences in moral development. "Each individual child must go step by step through each of the kinds of moral judgment outlined. It is, of course, possible for a child to move at varying speeds and to stop (become 'fixated') at any level of development, but if he continues to move upward, he must move in accord with these steps." (Kohlberg, 1971). Kohlberg maintains that these moral stages are independent of culture and religions. "All individuals in all cultures go through the same order or sequences of gross stages of development, although varying in rate and terminal point of development." "Maturity of moral judgment is correlated with cognitive maturity but is clearly distinguishable from it." "All morally advanced children are bright, but not all bright children are morally advanced."

Kohlberg described six stages of moral development. Stages one and two are considered *Preconventional Morality*. In these two stages the child's primary motivation is to avoid punishment and to receive reward. It is all about what is best for the self. At stage one a response to the Heinz dilemma might be that he shouldn't steal the drug because he'll go to jail. The fact that he was to suffer as the result makes the act wrong. Morality is something external to oneself. "It's wrong because it's against the law."

At stage two there is a recognition that there is more than one point of view. The main focus though is still on self-interest. In stage one it is punishment that *proves* an act is wrong. In stage two punishment is a risk that one naturally wants to avoid but it doesn't prove that the act is wrong. A response in stage 2 to the Heinz dilemma might be "Heinz might steal the drug if he wants his wife to live, but he doesn't have to if he wants to marry someone younger."

Stages three and four are considered *Conventional Morality*. Here the emphasis is on abeyance to social rules. At this level there is no distinction between moral principles and legal principles. What authority says is right and wrong *is* what is right and wrong. In western societies, individuals frequently enter stage three morality about the time they are entering their teens. The focus is on being a *good* person and living up to expectations of society. In stage three of this level the focus is on pleasing others and securing the favor of others. In stage four there is increased concern for society as a whole. "What would happen if we all started breaking the law if we felt we had good reason?!" This is a law and order morality. Kohlberg believed that many people remain in this stage for the rest of their lives; they derive principles of morality from society or religious leaders. They never learn to reason about moral principles on their own.

The third level of moral development is *Post-Conventional*. Here the concern is with universal moral values that transcend societal rules. People at this level begin to think about morality more theoretically. Morality and human "rights" takes precedence over particular laws. People begin to reason about what societies should value. In stage five of this level conceptions of morality become more *principled*. "Because conventional morality is not fully universal and prescriptive, it leads to continual self-contradictions, to definitions of right which are different for Republicans and Democrats, for Americans and Vietnamese, for fathers and sons. In contrast, principled morality is directed to resolving these conflicts in a stable, self-consistent fashion." (Kohlberg, 1971)

In stage six there is a realization that democratic processes do not always lead to justice. The United States Declaration of Independence, Constitution and the Bill of Rights were written to protect human rights and to promote justice. The U.S. Declaration of Independence says that we all have rights that are self-evident and that "all men are created equal, that they are endowed by their Creator with certain unalienable Rights, that among these are Life, Liberty and the pursuit of Happiness." These rights should supersede any particular laws. The Fourteenth Amendment to the U.S. Constitution requires that states provide the same rights, privileges and protections to all of its citizens. Because laws can be written by groups who want to restrict rights of certain groups, we have a Supreme Court to protect these rights. It was the Supreme Court that was primarily responsible for ending racial segregation. It was the Supreme Court who struck down state laws that prohibited inter-racial marriages. It was the Supreme Court that ruled that under the fourteenth amendment that state laws cannot discriminate against women (Reed v Reed in 1971). It was the Supreme Court that ruled that states could not prohibit gay marriage.

It is my opinion that it is extremely important to have government leaders who are *Post-Conventional* in their level of moral development and is particularly important for our Supreme Court judges. When citizens are at Pre-conventional and conventional levels of moral development, they don't care that some of their fellow citizens are discriminated against. It is either because it does not benefit them (pre-conventional) or they think it is better for society (conventional). Post-conventional morality is concerned about justice for all. Kohlberg (1971) said "At stage 1 only important persons' lives are valued, at stage 3 only family members, at stage 6 all life has equal moral value." "Because conventional morality is not fully universal and prescriptive, it leads to continual self-contradictions, to definitions of right which are different for Republicans and Democrats, for Americans and Vietnamese, for fathers and sons. In contrast, principled morality is directed to resolving these conflicts in a stable, self-consistent fashion."

For Kohlberg, stage 6 is about a clear awareness of universal principles and an emphasis on justice for all. Kohlberg conceptualized an even higher stage of moral development, a stage 7. "Its essence is the sense of being a part of the whole of life and the adoption of a cosmic, as opposed to a universal humanistic (Stage 6) perspective." (Kohlberg, 1990). It is a "shift from figure to ground". It seeks to find answers to the question about the meaning of life for those at higher stages of moral development.

"Figure-ground" has to do with perception. With vision our brain works to perceive a figure from its background. Sometimes that is hard to do, like in the example below. Is the figure a vase (in white), or is the figure two faces looking at each other (in black)?

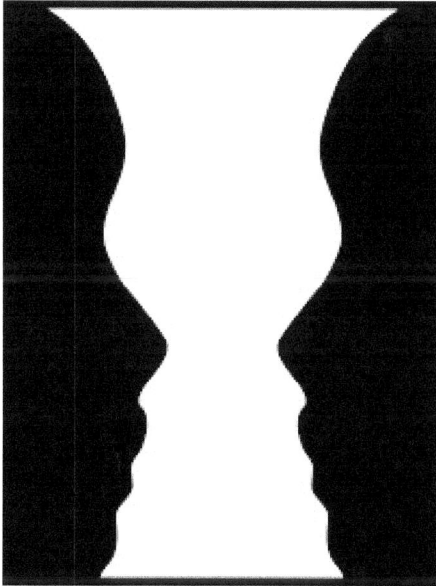

With stage 7 morality, Kohlberg said in regards to "figure" that "we are the self seen from the distance of the cosmic or infinite. In the state of mind I metaphorically term Stage 7, we identify ourselves with the cosmic or infinite perspective and value life from its standpoint. Spinoza, a believer in principled ethics and in a science of natural laws, described this state of mind as the 'union of the mind with the whole of nature.'" (Kohlberg, 1990).

This is the concept I shared earlier with the story from *Tuesdays with Morrie* about the little wave who is discovering that he is essentially part of the ocean and not really a wave. Mystics who are accomplished at meditation report that the illusion of individuality melts away during meditation. All figures become ground. All *parts* are components of the *whole*.

Sex Differences in Moral Reasoning

The reader might be reminded that all of Kohlberg's research was with male respondents. Is there a difference in moral development for females? Carol Gilligan (1982) maintains there is. Gilligan was a student of Kohlberg who maintains that women and men are different in that for males there is an emphasis on justice while for women there is more of a focus on caring. Gilligan reports that boys tend to emphasize independence, autonomy, and justice in their moral reasoning. In contrast, she reports that girls place more emphasis on relationships and care of others rather than independence. Gilligan developed her own stage theory of moral development, which like Kohlberg, is in three stages. As with Kohlberg, in stage one the child is completely self-centered. There then is a transition from selfishness to responsibility. In stage two there is reliance on others and the quest for social acceptance. The child focuses on being "good" to be socially accepted. Then there is a transition from "goodness" to truth. The individually no longer sacrifices the truth to be accepted by others. In stage three there is a focus on non-violence. There is emphasis on not hurting others and also on not hurting oneself.

The work of both theorists fit in well with my own contention that morality is a continuum from complete self-centeredness and selfishness to extravagant altruism. For both theorists stage one is about selfishness and self-centeredness. Stage two is about taking a broader perspective, incorporating societal values, and a need to be perceived as being "good". Stage three is concerned with the application of universal moral principles, to avoid violence, to care for others, and to be just. Although Kohlberg emphasizes justice, and Gilligan emphasizes caring, they are two sides to the same coin. Joseph Fletcher (1966) opines "Love and justice are the same, for justice is love distributed, nothing else." If you love and care for someone, you want to be just and fair. If you seek justice for people, it is because you care for them.

Both love and justice are the sentiments clearly expressed in the various manifestations of the "golden rule" (shared at the beginning of this book) and expressed by the great religious prophets.

Another Viewpoint on Morality

Psychologist Jonathan Haidt (2012) contends that "morality is like cuisine: it's a cultural construction, influenced by accidents of environment and history". Different people have different "taste buds". Just as some people like bitter tastes, others spicy, and others sweet, Haidt maintains that people have different preferences for morality. Haidt identifies five *moral foundations*. The first two are what Kohlberg and Gilligan have identified: care and fairness. Haidt adds loyalty, authority, and sanctity.

Haidt further supposes that the ideological left primarily relies on care and fairness as moral foundations, while the ideological right uses all five. I never realized where the terms "left" and "right" in regards to political ideology came from until I read Haidt's book. The terms originated in France during the French Revolution in 1789. At the legislative assembly delegates who were innovators sat on the left, moderates gathered in the center, and those who favored preservation sat on the right. Since then "right" came to be associated with conservatism, and "left" came to stand for liberalism.

One might think that the development of liberal or conservative ideology depends a great deal on upbringing. However, consistent with much of the research previously presented in this book, genetics appears to be the more important factor. Hatemi *et al.* (2011) report that evidence had been gathering for over 40 years for a genetic influence on political attitudes. Their study looking at the DNA of 13,000 people was consequential in finding several genes that differentiated between conservatives and liberals. "Most of them related to neurotransmitter functioning, particularly glutamate and serotonin, both of which are involved in the brain's response to threat and fear. This finding fits well with many studies showing that conservatives react more strongly than liberals to signs of danger, including the threat of germs and contamination, and even low-level threats such as sudden blasts of white noise. Other studies have implicated genes related to receptors for the neurotransmitter dopamine, which has long been tied to sensation-seeking and openness to experience, which are among the best-established correlates of liberalism." (Haidt, 2012).

Haidt states that humans have two competing motives. Neophilia is an attraction to new things, and neophobia is the fear of new things. People vary on this continuum, i.e. whether more open or fearful of the new and novel. Haidt reports that liberals are more open to new experiences, while conservatives are more resistant to experiencing the unfamiliar. Conservatives "prefer to stick with what's tried and true, and they care a lot more about guarding borders, boundaries, and traditions." (Haidt, 2012).

This is consistent with my own experiences. I do a lot of traveling throughout the world, and it has been noticeable that the vast majority of other travelers from the United

States have been liberal in their politics, particularly when traveling to more unusual countries such as India, Peru, or South Korea. Is it that liberals are more likely to travel the world, or does travel make one have a more liberal ideology, or is it a combination of both (which is what I would suspect)?

Let me now explore the three moral foundations that Haidt says are important to conservatives but not liberals and are not part of Kohlberg's and Gilligan's conception of morality.

Authority

Haidt maintains that one relevant aspect of morality is the reliance on authority. Many animal species rely on an authority, the alpha male, to provide leadership in their communities. One of the earliest religious ideas to develop in prehistoric religion, as I discussed in *Evolution and Syncretism of Religion* was animism, the belief that all living and non-living things possessed a spirit. From there developed a belief in gods, and from there developed specialists to the spiritual world, shamans. who were authorities about the gods. As hunter-gatherers began to settle, bands of families grew into tribes, and a leader was required to keep order, the chief. Eventually civilizations developed which required a king or emperor. These rulers' authority was believed to have come from the gods.

Unfortunately, the type of individuals who are most drawn to these positions of authority are alpha males who crave power. These individuals frequently are more concerned with their own self-interests than they are with their subjects.

Many people are drawn to this type of personality as they appear strong and confidant. They are often charismatic.

The earliest religions, including Judaism, were primarily concerned with obeying authority. The earliest religious ritual was to make sacrifices to gods in order to please them and to obtain favors. Then, as civilizations developed, rules and laws became necessary to keep order. These laws came from God or God's representatives, the rulers. Many believe that to be moral, one needs to obey the authorities. This philosophy is stated well in Romans 13 (verses 1-7):

Let every person be subject to the governing authorities; for there is no authority except from God, and those authorities that exist have been instituted by God. Therefore whoever resists authority resists what God has appointed, and those who resist will incur judgment. For rulers are not a terror to good conduct, but to bad. Do you wish to have no fear of the authority? Then do what is good, and you will receive its approval; for it is God's servant for your good. But if you do what is wrong, you should be afraid, for the authority does not bear the sword in vain! It is the servant of God to execute wrath on the wrongdoer. Therefore one must be subject, not only because of wrath but also because of conscience. For the same reason you also pay taxes, for the authorities are God's servants, busy with this very thing. Pay to all what is due them- taxes to whom taxes are due, revenue to whom revenue is due, respect to whom respect is due, honor to whom honor is due.

Just recently while in the process of writing this book attorney general Jeff Sessions quoted these verses in response to criticism about the government's separation of children from their immigrant parents at the Mexican border. In other words, don't question the morality of separating children from their parents; rather, follow the alternative conception of morality to do what your government says. Old Testament prophets such as Amos, Micah, Isaiah and Jeremiah emphasized justice over rules and laws. Even Paul, who wrote the above passage from Romans goes on to say in that same chapter that love is what's ultimately important: "love is the fulfilling of the law". For Jesus also, it was love that was most important. "In everything do to others as you would have them do to you; for this is the law and the prophets." (Matthew 7:12).

I personally do not believe there is a smorgasbord of morality where the following of authority is on equal footing as love and justice. I believe that during World War II in Nazi Germany a soldier who follows orders and puts a Jewish person in the gas chamber is less moral than a soldier who defies orders to rescue Jewish people. Martin Luther King Jr. addresses this in his "Letter from a Birmingham Jail" in 1965:

One may well ask, 'How can you advocate breaking some laws and obeying others?' The answer lies in the fact that one has not only a legal but a moral responsibility to obey just laws. One has a moral responsibility to disobey unjust laws, though one must do so openly, lovingly and with a willingness to accept the penalty. An individual who breaks a law that conscience tells him is unjust, and accepts the penalty to arouse the conscience of the community, is expressing in reality the highest respect for law. An unjust law is a human law not rooted in eternal law and natural law. A law that uplifts human personality is just; one which degrades human personality is unjust.

Loyalty

Haidt also puts loyalty on the morality smorgasbord. Dante in his *Inferno* reserves the deepest level of hell for traitors to family, country, lords and benefactors. In my opinion the only things we should be loyal to are truth, justice and love (agape). Loyalty to anything else is to me vice, not virtue. When we are wrong we should acknowledge it. When our family is wrong, we should call them out. When our sports team is wrong, we should call them out. When our political party is wrong, we should call them out. When our country is wrong, we should call them out. Justice is about having the same rules, responsibilities, expectations, and conse-quences for everyone. We should not have double standards.

Some might advocate that we should always be "true to our school" or "defend our country" no matter what. Such loy-alty can be misplaced. Again getting back to the Nazi Ger-many example, if one's country is promoting evil one should stand up against it rather than remaining loyal to it. It is wrong, I believe, to follow a leader or a country *no matter what*. Values and ideals should be our lodestar, not a person or an organization. I am not willing to die for my country, but I am willing to give my life for democracy. Racism, misogyny, homophobia, classism, tribalism and xenophobia are ongoing scourges. They are the antithesis of morality.

Sanctity

The last of Haidt's five moral foundations is the continuum between the sacred and that which is disgusting. Let's take this latter dimension of disgust first. The Pentateuch, the books of law of the Old Testament, deals extensively with issues of cleanliness and purity. Some examples from the book of Leviticus:

* Chapter 11 of Leviticus describes what foods are "clean" and "unclean". Animals that are clean or "pure" are those animals that have split hooves and are cud chewers. Animals deemed unclean would include the pig and the camel. In regards to sea creatures, they must have fins and scales. This leaves out shrimp and lobsters among others. Flying insects are unclean, but jumping insects such as grasshoppers are clean.

* Chapter 12 of Leviticus discusses the purification of women after childbirth. If the woman bears a male child, she "shall be ceremonially unclean seven days", and if she bears a female child "she shall be unclean two weeks". This means she "shall not touch any holy thing" or come into the sanctuary during this period of time.

* Leviticus 13 and 14 deals with skin diseases, some of which were contagious. These diseases were not treated and monitored by doctors, but rather by the priests. If the priest deemed a person as unclean due to skin disease, the person was required to wear torn clothes and an unadorned head, to live outside of camp, and to declare themselves as unclean if they got near other people while walking about. It is a priest that can later declare a person as again clean or a dwelling as being clean.

* Leviticus 15 deals with bodily discharges. A woman is unclean during menstruation. After seven days she must make a sacrifice of two turtledoves or two pigeons. Men after discharging semen are unclean for seven days as well. "Every bed on which the one with the discharge lies shall be unclean; and everything on which he sits shall be unclean."

The chapter goes on in great detail about the contaminating effects of bodily discharges.

The Pentateuch of the Old Testament makes great distinction between that which is "holy" and that which is "unclean". The sociologist Emile Durkheim wrote that a central characteristic of religions has been the dichotomy between the sacred and the profane. So what does all of this have to do with today? To modern ears all of this sounds quite antiquated. However, the idea of sacredness is still relevant in today's society, particularly to conservatives according to Haidt. To many, marital vows are considered sacred. Burial grounds may be considered sacred. The American flag is considered by many to be sacred; to burn it is an act of desecration. That is why it induces such passion in so many people.

In terms of the "unclean" or profane, an important emotion is disgust, the feeling of revulsion. This emotional response is believed to be very important from an evolutionary standpoint; it keeps us from getting in contact with things or people which can cause cause disease. We usually respond with disgust to spoiled foods, vermin, maggots, visible signs of infection, and bodily products such as feces and vomit. This is a response that keeps us safer. This response can also happen with "out-groups" i.e. xenophobia (the fear of people perceived to be foreign or strange). "In ancestral environments, interaction with members of the in-group will generally have posed less risk of disease transmission than interaction with members of an out-group, as individuals will have possessed antibodies to many of the pathogens present in the former, in contrast to those prevalent among the latter." (Navarrete, C. & Fessler, D., 2006).

Navarrete and Fessler include information from William Graham Sumner (1906) about ethnocentrism: "Ethnocentrism is the technical name for this view of things where one's own group is the center of everything, and all others are scaled and rated with reference to it...Sentiments are produced to correspond. Loyalty to the in-group, sacrifice for it, hatred and contempt for outsiders, brotherhood within, war-likeness without-- all group together, common products of the same situation. Navarrete and Fessler go on to say "the inclination to view members of other ethnic groups as not quite human is a persistent theme in the ethnographic and historical literatures that record the dynamics of intergroup relations."

There is also research that supports the concept of *moral disgust*. Jonathan Haidt (2012) has written that conservatives and liberals differ in terms of moral disgust. "Liberals score higher on measures of *neophilia* (also known as 'openness to experience'), not just for new foods but also for new people, music, and ideas. Conservatives are higher on *neophobia*; they prefer to stick with what's tried and true, and they care a lot more about guarding borders, boundaries, and traditions." Conservatives score higher on xenophobia than liberals, and liberals score higher on xenophilia (affection for unknown/ foreign objects and people). There is research to support genetic influences on moral disgust, but social conditioning also is important. Neuroanatomically, it is the insula that is believed to be the important brain structure for the emotion of disgust.

The Enlightenment or the *Age of Reason* began in the 17th Century with the start of the scientific revolution. Enlightenment writers emphasized reason and the scientific method. The Enlightenment led to an emphasis on human rights, individual liberties, and democracy. Haidt writes, however, that moral thoughts arise for many people not from human reason but from our emotions, and the emotion of disgust is of much importance. You might have heard someone say in response to being told about a behavior someone did as "That's just wrong!" The response is an emotional reaction. If you were to ask the person why the behavior is wrong, they likely would employ reason to justify their emotional response. The philosopher David Hume famously stated that reason is a slave to the passions. Haidt agrees with this. This goes against mainstream enlightenment reasoning, i.e. that emotions should be subservient to reason.

As a cognitive psychologist, I certainly would agree that reason needs to be the master of emotions. Feelings are important. We need to be aware of what we are feeling. Neuroscientist Antonio Damasio (1994) has written about the importance of emotions to the ability to reason. However, a key tenet of cognitive therapy is that feelings come from thoughts. When we change the way we *think*, we change the way we *feel*. Irrational, self-defeating thoughts lead to psychological dysfunction.

Haidt conducted research at the University of Virginia where he was a professor on the topic of moral emotions and moral reasoning. He and his colleagues read stories about taboos to subjects like this one below:

Julie and Mark, who are sister and brother, are traveling together in France. They are both on summer vacation from college. One night they are staying alone in a cabin near the beach. They decide that it would be interesting and fun if they tried making love. At the very least it would be a new experience for each of them. Julie is already taking birth control pills, but Mark uses a condom too, just to be safe.

They both enjoy it, but they decide not to do it again. They keep that night as a special secret between them, which makes them feel even closer to each other. So what do you think about this? Was it wrong for them to have sex?

Only 20% of the subjects asked said it was okay for Mark and Julie to have sex together, but subjects struggled to give a reason to support their moral judgment. According to Haidt "People made moral judgments quickly and emotionally. Moral reasoning was mostly just a post hoc search for reasons to justify the judgments people had already made." So, Haidt believes that moral judgments are from intuition and not as the result of reasoning. The reasoning is used only to try to justify the intuitive response. *Rationalization* is employed rather than rational thought.

Unfortunately, I believe Haidt is right that moral decisions are often made emotionally rather than rationally, and the feeling of disgust often leads people to make these emotional judgments. A couple examples include inter-racial marriage and homosexuality. Because of an intuitive aversion, a feeling of disgust, people devise rationalizations to support their gut reactions. Science has been conclusive about homosexuality being innate and immutable in males; yet despite the evidence, many people never became comfortable with homosexuals until they got to know them personally. That is the way it usually works with prejudice; people generally lose their prejudices not by reason or evidence but due to changes in emotional reactions that come with familiarity.

There is a psychological phenomenon known as *mere-exposure effect*. The researcher most associated with this is social psychologist Robert Zajonc. Basically the phenomenon is that novel stimuli (such as people perceived as foreign or strange) elicits fear/avoidance responses. With repeated exposure these fears fade away. We are comfortable with that which feels familiar. We are more comfortable with those in our family, our churches, our political party, our neighborhoods, and we tend to incorporate the ideas of the people and groups for which we are familiar, particularly if we are individuals who do not have critical reasoning abilities.

The Continuum of Evil

My belief is that good and evil are on a continuum. At the far left of the bell curve is evil, which is psychopathology. It is not *normal*. At the very farthest extreme are the sadistic psychopaths, i.e. people who not only are completely self-centered with little love, empathy and sympathy for other people, but who also *enjoy* the pain and suffering of others. To the right of them on the bell curve are the psychopaths who are not sadistic. To the right of them are those who are impulsively violent; they hurt others without aforethought. Their deficits are still due to psychopathology including at times brain injuries and genetics.

In the middle of the bell curve are those who would be in the average (i.e. typical, normal) range. The left side of normal are those with *pre-conventional morality* (using Kohlberg's stages of moral development). When children begin the process or moral reasoning (usually around the age seven or eight), they are very self-centered. Good is what benefits me and bad is what causes pain. At this stage there is not empathy or concern about others. Some individuals never leave this stage, even as adults. In this stage as an adult, it is okay if I steal something, for example, if I can get away with it.

Usually around the end of middle childhood and the early teens, children develop *conventional* moral reasoning. At this level individuals incorporate societal norms and values. They want to be thought of as *good,* and they try to live up to the expectations of family, teachers, etc. There is a focus on subservience to authority. Again, many adults never move past this level or moral reasoning. These individuals are legalistic; they focus on following the letter of the law. There really continues to be a lack of moral *reasoning.* There is still a good deal of self-centeredness at this stage in that by following the rules and norms of society one doesn't get in trouble and others think positively of them.

When one moves into *post-conventional* morality, there is a requirement for more abstract thinking. Increased moral development requires increased cognitive development. There is a realization that there are universal moral principles, and it is more important to follow these principles than it often is to follow specific laws and rules, as these laws may be in contradiction to the more important principles. These would be individuals who subscribe to the slogan of "question authority". These would be individuals who subscribe to *civil disobedience* when required. Unjust laws that discriminate should be fought against. Love and justice are principles that should be adhered to rather than hateful and unjust laws.

Kohlberg has written about a stage 7. Kohlberg saw this stage 7 of morality as reflecting a sense of oneness with the cosmos. Merriam-Webster defines *cosmos* as "an orderly harmonious systematic universe". Morality involves justice and agape love, and the reason at this stage that we want to be moral is because of the knowledge that we are part of the whole; to take care of the whole is to care for ourselves.

Again I'll return to the metaphor from the story in *Tuesdays with Morrie* about the wave; the focus is no longer on taking care of the wave or a collection of waves, but rather on focusing on improving the quality of the water. There is realization of being part of the ocean.

Other researchers, mystics, and thinkers have also written about such an advanced stage of spiritual and moral development. One such person is developmental psychologist James Fowler (1995). In Fowler's schema, there are six stages of faith development. Stage one (Intuitive-Projective Faith) emerges in children between the ages of 2 and 7. Children at this age are magical thinkers. They are also very egocentric, and they have little ability to take the perspective of others. Faith at this stage is fantasy–filled and is influenced greatly by stories and by actions of significant others. At this stage are early awarenesses of death and sex. The second stage (Mythic-Literal Faith) usually begins around the ages of 7 or 8. Children at this age take on the stories, beliefs, and practices of their community. Authority and tradition are powerful influences. As the name of the stage identifies, it is a stage where stories and myths are taken literally.

Stage three (Synthetic-Conventional Faith) begins to occur as a result of cognitive conflicts and less literal thinking. The capacity for abstract thinking begins to develop in adolescence. During this stage ideologies may develop but there is still no systematic reflection. The stage is most evident in adolescence, but many adults remain at this stage, and the stage can become long-lasting or even permanent.

Stage four (Individuative-Reflective Faith) can begin to develop in young adulthood. Due to critical analysis, previous beliefs inculcated from family and community are questioned and modified. This requires some courage to think critically and independently. The goal is to create a rational world view. For some the transition to stage four can be in the early to mid 20s, but for others it is during the 30s or 40s if at all.

The majority of adults never reach stage five (Conjunctive Faith). During this stage "community" is seen less parochially, and expands to encompass all of humanity.

Stage Six of Fowler's schema is called *Universalizing Faith*. There is dedication to "an inclusive and fulfilled human community". There is a "radical commitment to justice and love and of selfless passion for a transformed world, a world made over not in their images, but in accordance with an intentionality both divine and transcendent." (Fowler, 1981).

Psychologist Abraham Maslow is well known for his *Hierarchy of Needs*. The most basic needs on his hierarchy are *physiological needs*, i.e. the need for food, shelter, and oxygen. Once these needs are met, the next level of needs become most important. These are *safety needs*, i.e. the need for security, order, and stability. The next level up are *belongingness needs*, i.e. the need for love and connection with others. The next level up is *self-esteem needs*. This is the need to accomplish things and be recognized for it. Fame and fortune can be included in this. At the top of Maslow's well-known pyramid are *self-actualization needs*. The bottom four levels are "deficit needs", meaning that if you feel you do not have enough of these needs at a certain level, you are motivated to rectify this. The fifth level, self-actualization needs, deals with "being needs" rather than "deficit needs". At this level we deal with self-fulfillment-the desire to be all that we can be. It is the need for personal growth and evolution.

In psychology textbooks that is where the hierarchy of needs ends- with self-actualization at the top of the pyramid. However, Maslow wrote about an even higher level: *self-transcendence needs*. It expresses the idea that people need to move to a focus and concern for other people to move to the highest level of human development. Instead of focus on ourselves, there is a need to move into higher levels of consciousness and to have concern for ever widening circles of care. It is a move to ever increasing selflessness.

Ken Wilber is an American philosopher who has written extensively about stages of spiritual development. He has written about ten basic levels of consciousness. These can be categorized into three phases of development: The Prepersonal (Preegoic) phase, the Personal (Egoic) phase, and the Transpersonal (Transegoic) phase. Levels 1-3 are Prepersonal levels, levels 4-6 our Personal levels, and levels 7-10 are Transpersonal levels. The levels of consciousness at the Prepersonal and Personal phases of Wilber's theory are very similar to the first 5 stages of Fowler's faith stages.

When a child is born the baby has no sense of self as being separate from the mother or the world. A child gradually becomes aware that they are an independent being. They become focused on their body and fulfilling bodily needs. The child expresses this awareness of autonomy by being defiant, a period known as the "terrible twos". Later, group belonging becomes dominant. There is an over identification with the ones' tribe. With the advent for the capacity of logical thinking (around the age of 8) there develops a reflective self-consciousness. And later there may develop the capacity for abstract thinking.

With further development an individual may move to *Transpersonal* levels of consciousness. Transpersonal psychology is a sub-field of psychology. It has been defined by Bruce Scotton (1996) as "development beyond conventional, personal or individual levels". "Trans-personal experiences" has been defined as experiences in which the sense of identity or self extends beyond (trans) the individual or personal to encompass wider aspects of humankind, life, psyche or cosmos." (Walsh & Vaughan, 1993).

Ken Wilber has been important in the development of this field of study, although in later years he has preferred the term "integral" to describe his philosophy rather than "trans-personal". Wilber stresses the importance of meditation in order to experience transpersonal reality, i.e. the capacity to transcend ego-based reality and the ability to embrace the awareness of the complete interdependence of everything in the Cosmos. In other words, the ability to see that every-thing is part of the one, and that we are not waves but are actually part of the ocean.

Accomplished practitioners of meditation report this aware-ness of the oneness of everything in the cosmos. Wilber describes stages in the development of this awareness; these are his four levels of transpersonal stage development, i.e. level 7 (psychic), level 8 (subtle), level 9 (causal), and level 10 (nondual). At this time I will not go into any more depth about these four levels. Jesus the Christ is believed by many to be an accomplished practitioner of meditation; many believe that his forty days and forty nights of fasting in the Judean desert was a time of deep meditation. Jesus in the Gospel of John (10:30) was quoted as saying "The father and I are one". Many take this verse to mean that Jesus is uniquely God. However, Jesus also was quoted in the Gospel of John as saying "the Father is greater than I" (14:28), and later in the Gospel as stating his wish that all may be one: "As you, father, are in me and I am in you, may they also be in us." (17:21).

Wilber stresses the importance of experiencing the oneness of the cosmos through the practices of meditation. I have not had this experience, but I can understand it and accept it based on reason alone. If I had another lifetime to live I would devote a significant amount of time to practicing meditation. I would love to have the experience of feeling in touch with God. What is more important for me then experiencing God is helping to bring forth the "Kingdom of God" which to me is hastening the evolution of the Cosmos.. It is about expanding the circle of morality.

Peter Singer in his book "The Expanding Circle" wrote about this. Singer includes the following quotation from the philosopher Henry Sidgwick:

We should all agree that each of us is bound to show kindness to his parents and spouse and children, and to other kinsmen in a less degree; and to those who have rendered services to him, and any others whom he may have admitted to his intimacy and called friends; and to neighbors and to fellow countrymen more than others; and perhaps we may say to those of our own race more than to black or yellow men, and generally to human beings in proportion to their affinity to ourselves.

Sidgwick was writing about the "duty of benevolence" known at that time in Victorian England. Singer writes that much of this still holds true. "We still think first of our immediate family, then of friends, neighbors, and more distant relatives, next to our fellow citizens generally and last of all to those who have nothing in common with us except that they are human beings." In other words, with this philosophy, what is important is that it is *mine*. I give precedence if it is *my* family. I give precedence if it is *my* neighbor. I give precedence if it is a member of *my* club. I give precedence if it is *my* country. Singer argues against this morality of selfishness. "Ethical reasoning, once begun, pushes against our initially limited ethical horizons, leading us always toward a more universal point of view." "Taking the impartial element and ethical reasoning to its logical conclusion means, first, accepting that we ought to have equal concern for all human beings." (Singer, 1981). Singer goes on to say that the moral circle should grow to include nonhuman animals. Singer includes this quote from Albert Schweitzer:

A man is really ethical only when he obeys the constraint laid on him to help all life which he is able to succour, and when he goes out of his way to avoid injuring anything living. He does not ask how far this or that life deserves sympathy as valuable in itself, nor how far it is capable of feeling. To him life itself is sacred.

On the next page is a figure depicting my conception of the continuum of morality. On the left are those who are considered evil- those who suffer from psychopathology. Most of the people are in the middle of the bell curve; those whose moral development would be considered "pre-conventional" or "conventional". To the right are those who are exceptionally morally developed, i.e. those at the "post-conventional" level of moral development and even further to the right at "transpersonal" or "integral".

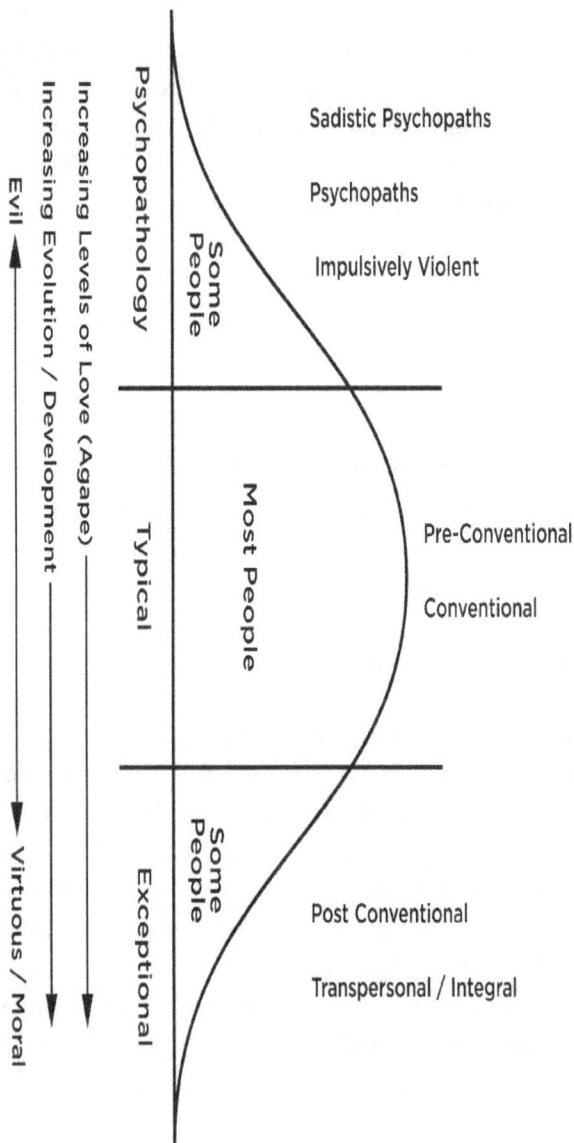

Continuum of Morality

Craig R. Vander Maas

To the left of the bell curve are those most selfish; to the right are those with the most expanded "circle of care", those who strive to extend the most love (agape). Now, let me make clear that those individuals who are furthest to the right are not those without faults. They still make mistakes. They still commit acts that are selfish and thoughtless. However, they have developed a moral paradigm in which they strive to be inclusive and loving.

Those that are evil certainly are responsible for much of the woe in the world. In fact, Steven Pinker (2011) maintains that tens of millions of deaths "ultimately depended on the decisions of just three individuals", i.e. Adolf Hitler, Joseph Stalin and Mao Zedong. However, perhaps even more of the woes of the world have been the result of actions of those in the middle of the bell curve, the average humans, who are willing to forego justice for others if it benefits themselves. The selfishness and self-centeredness of the average human being is, I believe, the essence of "sin"

In Freudian terms, it is our "id" that is the problem. Sigmund Freud saw the human psyche as consisting of three parts: the id, the ego, and the superego (Freud, 1923). The *id* operates on the *pleasure principle*, (Freud, 1920), i.e. the primitive and selfish drive to gain pleasure and to avoid pain. The newborn child has only this aspect in their psyche. As the child grows, they develop an *ego*; the ego also desires the fulfillment of pleasure, but it works on the *reality principle*. Reason is now employed to find acceptable and appropriate ways to obtain pleasure. The *superego* is concerned with morality. During the age of three to five the child begins to incorporate values and morals from their parents and others in society. The function of the superego is to contain the id's impulses and to persuade the ego to pursue moralistic goals, i.e. to think of others and not just oneself.

I believe it is the selfish striving to satisfy the pleasure principle and the lack of moral development of humanity that is the main cause for the woes of the world. It is the reason for wars and poverty. "The Hunger Project" reports that 821 million people are currently chronically malnourished in the world. "767 million people, or 1 in 10 people in the world, live on under $1.90 a day...328 million children are living in extreme poverty." Yet, another person was able to spend 3.12 million dollars for a Honus Wagner baseball card in 2016. Another person spent $14,740 in 2010 for a toilet belonging to John Lennon. Another person spent $29,900 for a piece of wedding cake from King Edward the 8th's wedding in 1937.

Income inequality is a growing problem in the United States and in the world, and many consider this a moral crisis. The income disparity in the United States is the greatest it has been since 1928 just prior to the Great Depression. Marriner Eccles chaired the Federal Reserve Board from 1934 until 1948, and the Federal Reserve Board is now housed in a building named after him in Washington, DC. Eccles concluded that the major cause of the Great Depression "had nothing whatever to do with excessive spending during the 1920s. It was, rather, the vast accumulation of income in the hands of the wealthiest people in the nation, which siphoned purchasing power away from most of the rest" (Reich, 2013).

An article in the Washington Post on December 6, 2017 titled "The richest 1 percent now owns more of the country's wealth than at any time in the past 50 years" stated that the wealthiest 1 percent owns 40% of the country's wealth. An article in Forbes (Nov. 9, 2017) maintains that just three individuals, Bill Gates, Warren Buffett and Jeff Bezos, collectively have more wealth than the bottom 50% of the U.S. population (160 million people). Forbes information comes from a report published by the Institute for Policy Studies. One of the authors said "If left unchecked, wealth will continue to accumulate into fewer and fewer hands, a trend we've been witnessing for decades."

I'm sure that Gates, Buffett, Bezos and the other billionaires in the United States are very smart and hard working, but not millions of times smarter or hardworking than those in the bottom fifty percent of the population. Reich (2013) reports that "money has translated into large campaign donations to politicians who do the bidding of their wealthy patrons-reducing their tax rates, widening tax loopholes, gaining government subsidies and bailouts for their businesses, and slashing regulations that impinge on them but would otherwise protect the public." Reich, however, is a capitalist and realist: "Let me be clear. Some inequality is inevitable; we are not born with equal talents and inherited abilities. Some inequality is also necessary if people are to have adequate incentive to work hard, invent, and innovate to the benefit of everyone." Writing in the early 2000s, Reich also appears quite prescient writing that "at some point inequality becomes so wide it causes a society to fracture. Average people become so frustrated and fearful they become easy prey for demagogues hurling blame at anyone or any group that's a convenient scapegoat".

Part of humanity's "sin" is not just to avoid pain and to maximize pleasure, but also to feel superior to others. Competition can be positive in some ways such as encouraging innovation and progress, but it has significant downsides as well.

Materialism to a large extent is more than just receiving pleasure. It is about advertising to the world one's financial success. Is driving an automobile that costs hundreds of thousands of dollars or even millions of dollars more pleasurable than driving an automobile that costs a few thousand? It's all about projecting social status. Another downside of competition is the tendencies of many to not only elevate ourselves above others but to denigrate others. Not only do we want to be *winners*, but we want others to be *losers*. The recent upsurge in the "White Supremacy" movement is a good example. The ideology of these white people is that they are inherently superior to people of color. Contrast this to the "Black Lives Matter" movement; the ideology of this movement is not that black lives matter and others don't, but rather that black lives matter *too*.

Racism, sexism, heterosexism, ageism, and classicism are all about power and control by one segment of society over others. By keeping some elements of society down we think that we are elevating ourselves. Somehow we think it is a zero-sum game. Baseball is a zero-sum game; not only do we want to score as many runs as possible, but we also want the other team to score as few runs as possible. Much of life is often not a zero-sum game however. We have learned that often we benefit if others benefit too. International trade has been a good example of this. Rather than thinking in terms of winners and losers, we have learned that trade can be a positive sum game, i.e. that there are no losers and that all parties can win in the exchange.

Many evil acts have been done by average human beings, those in the middle of the morality bell curve. A good example is slavery, an evil that occurred in our own country not that long ago. Just imagine having no freedoms, not being able to pursue your dreams, not being able to marry but maybe being forced to breed, being separated from loved ones at any time, and being vulnerable to ongoing physical and verbal abuse and rape. This evil was perpetrated by average Americans who did not want to lose their lifestyles. The plantations of the south could not continue without conscribed labor. Of course these "good people" wouldn't admit to themselves or others that they were doing evil, and so they would come up with rationalizations, such as "slaves don't have the ability to live on their own and so it's best for them if someone else controls their lives", or "since they're really not fully human, slavery is no more wrong than having domestic animals that do work", or "it's part of God's plan and is endorsed in the Bible". These were average, often church-going Americans. It was the issue of slavery that caused the Southern Baptist church (who advocated ongoing slavery) to split off from the Baptist Church in 1845.

This selfishness and self-centeredness is the antithesis of the ideology expressed in the Golden Rule. Instead of doing to others what we would like done for us, the prevailing creed seems to be to do for ourselves whatever we want without concern about the welfare of others. During the Axial Age, there was an evolution in moral thought. This is when the sentiments of the Golden Rule arose in many religions. Clearly, though, it is too infrequently followed. Hopefully with further evolution of human spirituality it will eventually become the norm.

Chapter 4

How Should We Then Live?

In my 20s I read a book by the Swiss evangelical theologian Francis Schaeffer entitled "*How Should We Then Live*". What I appreciated about the book even back then was attempts to answer questions of morality and finding answers to the title of the book. I also appreciated Schaeffer's attempts to provide a comprehensive and coherent world view. However, his worldview, and the worldview of most Christian theologians, is based upon what I believe is a faulty assumption, i.e. that the Bible is the *literal* word of God. These theologians subscribe to the *doctrine of inerrancy* which means that the Bible is completely without error and *presuppositional apologetics* which means that one defends the Christian beliefs with the presupposition that the Bible is divine revelation.

It is my experience that most Christians have little knowledge about the Bible and why it should be considered the literal words of God. Muslims would tell you that God spoke to Muhammad through the angel Gabriel and the Quran was dictated to the prophet. Mormons would tell you that the Book of Mormon was written by prophets in an unknown language on golden plates. The angel Moroni translated the writing for the religious leader Joseph Smith. Both of these religious groups have a narrative to explain the divine revelations they believe in. Christians have no ready narratives to explain their beliefs. I find that evangelical Christians cite a belief in the infallibility of the Bible without any knowledge about the history of the development of the Bible. That is why I chose to write in the first book of this series information about the development of the Bible. It is clear to me that the Bible *evolved* rather than was *revealed*. It is also clear to me that all the religions evolved rather than were revealed. The evidence for this is the information I presented in book two of this series.

A literal reading of the Bible allows adherents to pick out obscure passages to support otherwise untenable positions. If one believes that a writing is the direct word of God, then every sentence is of importance. It allows Muslims to find support for jihad. It allows Christians to find support for all types of evil including racial prejudice, xenophobia, slavery and genocide (although if one were to look at other passages of the Bible one would find condemnations of the above).

A non-literal but serious reading of the Bible reveals trends and important developing themes. The Bible teaches that the earliest followers of gods including Yahweh primarily were interested in appeasing gods with sacrifices so that the gods would look favorably upon them. A further development in religion, including with the religion of the Israelite people, was the establishment of laws; Moses was the great law-giver. This was a necessary development as tribes grew to become larger civilizations. During the Axial Age the Hebrew prophets began to stress justice rather than sacrifices and ritual. I discussed this important historical period in some detail in my previous books. It was during this historical period that morality became important in religion.

The New Testament scholar Marcus Borg 1994) said that we do not know a great deal about the historical Jesus, but he does report six things that scholars mostly agree on:

1. The message of Jesus was *theocentric,* not *christocentric*. In other words, Jesus focused on the importance of God, not on himself.

2. Scholars have come to believe that Jesus was *noneschatological*, which means that Jesus did not believe in a "supernatural coming of the Kingdom of God as a world-ending event in his own generation."

3. Jesus was a *spirit person*. Jesus likely meditated and experienced the presence of God.

4. Jesus was a *teacher of wisdom*. "Basically, wisdom concerns how to live. It speaks of the nature of real-ity and how to live one's life in accord with reality." Borg discusses two types of wisdom: conventional wisdom is the common wisdom and beliefs of a cul-ture. Borg said Jesus taught an alternative wisdom (as did Lao-tzu and Buddha before him). Jesus' wis-dom undermined conventional wisdom. For exam-ple, Jesus said "You have heard that it was said 'you shall love your neighbor and hate your enemy.' But I say to you, Love your enemies and pray for those who persecute you, so that you may be children of your Father in heaven".

5. Jesus was a *social prophet*. He criticized the politi-cal and social systems of his time and those in authority.

6. Jesus was a *movement founder*.

So what was this movement? What was the essential teach-ings of Jesus that he thought were important for changing the world? Jesus taught an ethic of compassion (i.e. empathy, sympathy and love). It was an ethic of inclusivity. Jesus reached out to the marginalized in that society, e.g. women, the poor, children, Samaritans, tax collectors, the "untouch-ables". As the apostle Paul stated in Galatians 3:28, "There is no longer Jew or Greek, there is no longer slave or free, there is no longer male and female; for all of you are one in Christ Jesus."

Borg also talked about the culture of that day (as well as our own) as being a culture of selfishness. "Its dominant values are what I call the three A's- achievement, affluence, and appearance. We live our lives in accord with these values, with both our self-worth and level of satisfaction dependent upon how well we measure up to these culture messages." Jesus, on the other hand, advocated a life of other-centered-ness- a focus on the love of God and others. So in answer to the question of "how should we then live?", the answer is a life of love of God and love for others. It is a matter of seek-ing justice for all. It is living the "golden rule. This is the evolutionary arc of all the great religions. What's more, when we do live our lives with concern for others and not just ourselves, the whole world benefits.

Non-zero sum world

I mentioned the term "zero-sum" earlier. "Zero-sum" means that my gain is someone else's loss, and my loss is someone else's gain. Baseball, as I mentioned previously, is a zero-sum game. The other team's gains of runs is my team's loss, and my gain of runs is the other team's loss. By gaining more than the other team, my team wins. Some people look at life this way. I want other people to lose, as I see it as my gain. This outlook is the antithesis of the "golden rule". Rozycka-Tran, et al (2015) defined zero-sum thinking: "a general belief system about the antagonistic nature of social relations, shared by people in a society or culture and based on the implicit assumption that a finite amount of goods exists in the world, in which one person's winning makes others the loser, and vice versa."

Zero-sum thinking is a major contributor to wars. Countries start wars in order to gain natural resources such as oil or minerals, or to gain land for expansion, or to gain access to a body of water. In this case our country's gain is the other country's loss. Wars are also started because of hatred toward others. We hate others because of their ethnicity or their religion. In this case, their loss is our gain. If we learn from history, however, we see that there really are not winners with war in the long run. War interferes with the evolution of our species. Positive-sum solutions are possible. There doesn't necessarily have to be winners and losers. In the long run it is possible to have outcomes in which all parties gain. Robert Wright (2000) in his book *Non Zero: The Logic of Human Destiny* writes "Non-zero-sumness is a kind of potential- a potential for overall gain, or for overall loss, depending on how the game is played." "Non-zero-sumness, I'll argue, is something whose ongoing growth and ongoing fulfillment define the arrow of the history of life, from the primordial soup to the World Wide Web."

World War I ended with the Treaty of Versailles, which required Germany to pay extravagant sums of money in war reparations. Also, England and France were asked by the Americans for compensation for their assistance during the war. These countries could not afford to pay this. Their economies were bankrupt. They also could not afford to buy United States goods, and this contributed to the worldwide Great Depression. The economic burden of the Treaty of Versailles is believed to be a contributing factor to the receptiveness of the German people to Hitler and subsequently to World War II.

At the end of World War II a different approach was taken. Rather than following the age old paradigm of war in which it is a zero-sum game, i.e. to the victors go the spoils and the defeated lie vanquished, the "Marshall Plan" was enacted. It was an American initiative that involved giving over 13 billion in 1948 dollars to rebuilding Europe. This was an incredible amount of money and unheard of generosity; after four years of war the United States helped the country that was responsible for the deaths of hundreds of thousands of its citizens. The unique plan was a tremendous success. It staved off starvation and political upheaval. It prevented the spread of Russian communism into western Europe. It forged alliances between European countries and America which developed into NATO a year later.

I believe we need to evolve from the old paradigm of "winners and losers". Selfishness in the long run is a losing strategy. Putting into practice the Golden Rule is in the long run a winning strategy for all. The Treaty of Versailles was an example of zero-sum thinking; the results were not good. The Marshall Plan was an example of non-zero-sum thinking; that investment helped usher in 70 years of unprecedented economic prosperity for the United States and no World War III.

The conventional wisdom at the time of Jesus was as it is today: a life of selfishness and self-preoccupation. We compete with others in what Borg called the three A's- achievement, affluence, and appearance. Selfishness is the opposite of love, which is the extending of oneself for the benefit of *others*. Jesus primarily advocated the love of God and others, rather than trying to best others. Surprisingly, and ironically, I believe that we end up benefiting more ourselves when we live lives that follow the Golden Rule. I believe the apostle Paul's writing about the body of Christ in First Corinthians 12 has some relevance:

12 For just as the body is one and has many members, and all the members of the body, though many, are one body, so it is with Christ. 13 For in the one Spirit we were all baptized into one body—Jews or Greeks, slaves or free—and we were all made to drink of one Spirit.

14 Indeed, the body does not consist of one member but of many. 15 If the foot would say, "Because I am not a hand, I do not belong to the body," that would not make it any less a part of the body. 16 And if the ear would say, "Because I am not an eye, I do not belong to the body," that would not make it any less a part of the body. 17 If the whole body were an eye, where would the hearing be? If the whole body were hearing, where would the sense of smell be? 18 But as it is, God arranged the members in the body, each one of them, as he chose. 19 If all were a single member, where would the body be? 20 As it is, there are many members, yet one body. 21 The eye cannot say to the hand, "I have no need of you," nor again the head to the feet, "I have no need of you." 22 On the contrary, the members of the body that seem to be weaker are indispensable, 23 and those members of the body that we think less honorable we clothe with greater honor, and our less respectable members are treated with greater respect; 24 whereas our more respectable members do not need this. But God has so arranged the body, giving the greater honor to the inferior member 25 that there may be no dissension within the body, but the members may have the same care for one another. 26 If one member suffers, all suffer together with it; if one member is honored, all rejoice together with it.

Paul is explaining that just like the human body which has different parts for different functions, so it is for the "body of Christ". All of the parts are important. The "body" is the

Christian Church, and Paul says that individuals have different gifts to contribute, e.g. teaching, healing, speaking in
tongues, etc. The next chapter of First Corinthians is Paul's
famous chapter on love. He reports that love (agape) is the
most "excellent way".

I believe these two chapters of Paul apply to all of
humankind, and indeed to the entire biosphere. All of life is
important. It makes no more sense to harm another human
being than it does for me to cut off my left arm in service to
my right arm. The "body" of humankind is indeed one.
Again, going back to the metaphor about the wave, we are
not individual waves but rather we are the ocean. Returning
to the words of Paul: *If one member suffers, all suffer
together with it; if one member is honored, all rejoice
together with it.* What I'm talking about is a transpersonal
viewpoint.

The corruption of Christianity

Jesus' message is about love of God and others. It is a message against selfishness and self-centeredness. It is a message of radical inclusiveness. Ironically, Christianity to a
large extent has become the antithesis of this message.
While the early stories about Jesus describes his sacrificing
his life for his ideas and for others, a theology developed
over time known as *substitutionary atonement*. Thanks to
Anselm of Canterbury, a Catholic theologian and monk, this
theology became dominant in the church in the early Middle
Ages.. Its premise goes back to one of the earliest religious
conceptions, i.e. the need to make a sacrifice to God(s) in
order to make amends. Jesus' death is seen as a sacrifice by
God of his only son (just like Abraham was prepared to do of

his son Isaac) in order to pay a debt. The debt is for the sins of mankind.

Theologian Marcus Borg (1994) opines "The notion that God's only son came to this planet to offer his life as a sacrifice for the sins of the world, and that God could not forgive us without that having happened, and that we are saved by believing this story, is simply incredible."

Psychologist Steven Pinker's comments (2011) on this are even more pointed: "Though infinitely powerful, compassionate, and wise, he [God] could think of no other way to reprieve humanity from punishment for its sins (in particular, for the sin of being descended from a couple who had disobeyed him) than to allow an innocent man (his son no less) to be impaled through the limbs and slowly suffocate in agony. By acknowledging that this sadistic murder was a gift of divine mercy, people could earn eternal life. And if they failed to see the logic in all this, their flesh would be seared by fire for all eternity."

Over time somehow the requirement for "salvation" moved from following the law, then to "grace" (an unearned gift of God), and then to holding *correct* beliefs. For many people who self-identify as Christians the main goal is to go to Heaven after death and to avoid Hell. This is a very selfish and self-centered religious idea. The concern is only about self.

In recent years another theology has developed that focuses on self-aggrandizement. It is called *prosperity theology*. It is a minority Christian viewpoint that postulates that God wants his faithful followers to prosper with health and wealth. Oral Roberts was an early proponent of this theology, and it was popular with televangelists starting in the

1960s. These television preachers promised that if people donated to their ministries, they would be blessed with health and wealth several fold. Preacher Joel Osteen has been a recent advocate of this theology.

For many Christians prayer has also become self-centered. Jesus recommended in the famous "Lord's Prayer" to pray "*Your* will be done on earth as it is in Heaven". Instead, how often do we pray for *our* will to be done? And instead of focusing on praying for others, how often do we pray for ourselves, particularly for our wealth and health? God has often become to many the equivalent of a Santa Claus. Children write letters to Santa Claus asking for toys and other material goods. For how many of us as we became adults did we simply substitute God for Santa Claus? God, please help me get this new job. God, please help me get that raise. God, please help me to lose weight. God please help me get accepted into that school. God please help my football team win this afternoon.

Christianity has also become a religion of exclusivity. Many believe in a strict dichotomy of those who are "in", i.e. "saved", and those who are "out" or "lost". Those who hold correct beliefs are "in". Those who are diseased or poor are probably "out" if one subscribes to the above prosperity theology. Homosexuals are "out". Those who are "out" are punished for eternity in Hell, whereas those in the "in"-group are rewarded in Heaven.

Does all of this sound like Jesus? Jesus was inclusive of the outcasts. He taught extravagant love. He said "blessed are the poor". He taught a morality that gained prominence during the Axial Age and has been taught by all the great religious prophets since. Research suggests that as individuals evolve morally and spiritually there is a movement away

149

from self-centeredness and a movement toward more other-centeredness and inclusiveness. That, I believe, is "how we should then live"

Humanity is evolving

There has been progress for humanity in moral development. It is beneficial to look at humanity's history, and that is just what psychologist Steven Pinker (2011) did and published in his outstanding book *The Better Angels of our Nature*. Many believe in the myth of the "noble savage", i.e. the belief that before civilizations developed the hunter gatherers were a nomadic and peaceful people and violent acts were minimal. As I wrote in the first chapter of this book, that was not the case at all, and hominid species that predated our own also were likely very violent. Pinker, whose book is loaded with data, looked at the rates of violence between nonstate societies (i.e. not ruled by an organized government) and civilized societies. When looking at relative numbers and not absolute numbers (i.e. the percentage of populations), we see that the nonstate societies were the much more violent. In looking at the remains of hunter-gathers (prior to state societies) that date from 14,000 BCE to 1770 CE the rates of violent death range from 0 to 60 percent "with an average of 15 percent". In looking at eight recent hunter-gather societies, the average is a similar 14 percent. In contrast, although there were 40 million battle deaths in the 20th century and 180 million deaths (if we add genocides, purges, and other "man-made disasters"), that amounts to only about 3 percent (in contrast to the 14 to15 percent in hunter-gather societies).

In the earliest civilizations wars were common, and the victors were very cruel to their captives. The Hebrew scriptures tell of their own captivity by the Babylonians, and their writings also acknowledge cruelty themselves of peoples of other nations, For example, Joshua 6:21 states that the Israelites invaded the city of Jericho and they "devoted to destruction by the edge of the sword all in the city, both men and women, young and old, oxen, sheep, and donkeys."

King Ashurnasirpal II of Assyria was known to be particularly barbaric. He wrote *"Many captives from among them I burned with fire, and many I took as living captives. From some I cut off their noses, their ears and their fingers, of many I put out the eyes. I made one pillar of the living and another of heads, and I bound their heads to tree trunks round about the city. Their young men and maidens I burned in the fire."*

Also human sacrifice was common before the common era in the "old world" (and occurred many centuries later in the "new world"). I wrote quite extensively about human sacrifice in the ancient Mediterranean world in *Evolution and Syncretism of Religion*. The sacrifice of children was particularly common. Infanticide "of both legitimate and illegitimate children was a regular practice of antiquity, that the killing of legitimate children was only slowly reduced during the Middle Ages, and that illegitimate children continued regularly to be killed right up into the nineteenth century" (Demause, 1982). Demause reports that the history of childhood in general "is a nightmare from which we have only recently begun to awaken. The further back in history one goes, the lower the level of child care, and the more likely children are to be killed, abandoned, beaten, terrorized, and sexually abused."

During the Roman period two examples of cruelty included the Colosseum and crucifixion. The Colosseum was a stadium in which various grand spectacles of gore were a source of entertainment. The Roman public appears to have enjoyed seeing people ripped apart and eaten by animals. There were fights between gladiators to the death. Pinker (2011) reports that a half million people died agonizing deaths in the Colosseum for the entertainment of the Roman populace. Most people know that Jesus was crucified by the Romans, and this barbarous method of execution was common. The procedure was to first flog the prisoner, and then the prisoner would carry his 100 lb. cross to the site where he was to be crucified. He then would be nailed to the cross through the wrists and feet. The weight of the person's body would cause the rib cage to be distended making it difficult to breathe. It might take three or four days before the person would die from asphyxiation or blood loss.

With the fall of the Western Roman Empire came the Middle Ages or Medieval period. Pinker (2011) writes that "medieval Christendom was a culture of cruelty." He goes on to say:

"Executions were orgies of sadism, climaxing with ordeals of prolonged killing such as burning at the stake, breaking on the wheel, pulling apart by horses, impalement through the rectum, disembowelment by winding a man's intestines around a spool, and even hanging, which was a slow racking and strangulation rather than a quick breaking of the neck. Sadistic tortures were also inflicted by the Christian church during its inquisitions, witch hunts, and religious wars. Torture had been authorized by the ironically named Pope Innocent IV in 1252, and the order of Dominican monks carried it out with relish."

This type of unspeakable torture for the most part has become a thing of the past. Even during times of war, torture has been condemned. The Geneva Conventions of 1949 prohibited "torture and other cruel or inhuman treatment and outrages upon personal dignity, in particular humiliating and degrading treatment." These prohibitions are also cited by the United Nations.

World War II is unsurpassed in regards to wars and massacres in regards to the death toll. Fifty-five million people died in this horrendous event. However, when we scale the death toll to the world population at the time of the event, WW-II comes in at Number 9, according to Pinker (2011). Here are the events surpassing WW-II (Pinker's data, 2011): These figures include not only battlefield deaths but also indirect deaths due to starvation and disease.

1. This was the An Lushan Revolt against the Tang Dynasty in China in the 8th century. The death toll was 36 million people, which scaled to its mid-20th century equivalent would be 429 million people. A sixth of the world's population died.

2. Mongol invasions and conquests in the 13th century. Forty million people died, which scaled to its mid-20th century equivalent would be 278 million people.

3. Mideast Slave Trade from the 7th to 19th centuries. Nineteen million people died which scaled to its mid-20th century equivalent would be 132 million people.

4. Fall of the Ming Dynasty in the 17th century. Twenty-five million people died which scaled to its

mid-20th century equivalent would be 112 million people.

5. Fall of Rome from the 3rd to 5th centuries. Eight million people died which scaled to its mid-20th century equivalent would be 105 million people.

6. Timur Lenk was a Turco-Mongol conqueror in the 14th-15th centuries. Seventeen million people died which scaled to its mid-20th century equivalent would be 100 million people.

7. The annihilation of the American Indians from the 15th to the 19th centuries. Twenty million native Americans were killed which scaled to its mid-20th century equivalent would be 92 million people.

8. The Atlantic Slave Trade from the 15th to the 19th centuries. Slaves were brought from Africa to the American continent, and eighteen million died which scaled to its mid-20th century equivalent would be 83 million people.

Next on the list then comes World War II. The period of time since WWII has been termed "the long peace" by Steven Pinker and others. The reason is that this has been a remarkable period without significant military conflicts. Initially this was attributed to the cold war, but since the cold war ended the "long peace" has continued. Data has suggested that not only have military conflicts and deaths been down, but so has terrorism, genocide and homicide numbers. Pinker suggests that this has been part of a longer trend suggesting humanity has been becoming less violent and more moral.

This may be surprising to many people. There seems to be a misconception that we are living in particularly violent and degenerate times. Pinker (2011) noted, "When I surveyed perceptions of violence in an Internet questionnaire, people guessed that 20th-century England was about 14 percent more violent than 14th-century England. In fact it was 95 percent less violent."

Genocide (which is the deliberate killing of large groups of people because of their ethnicity or religion) and democide (the intentional killing of large groups of citizenry by its government) have been shockingly common throughout humanity's history. Rudolph Rummel was a political scientist who collected data on war and violence. He estimated that governments killed 133 million people before the 20th century (and the total may be as high as 625 million). The practice is particularly heinous in that innocent men, women and children are slaughtered not for what they did but for who they were. I mentioned earlier the slaughters by the Mongolians led by Genghis Khan in the 13th century (number 2 above) and by the Mongols under Timur Lenk in the 14th-15th centuries (number 6 above). Genocide did not end with the Mongols. It has even been perpetrated in America, i.e. the annihilation of the native peoples of America (number 7 above). Pinker (2011) wrote "Puritans in New England exterminated the Pequot nation in 1638, after which the minister Increase Mather asked his congregation to thank God 'that on this day we have sent six hundred heathen souls to Hell.' This celebration of genocide did not hurt his career. He later became president of Harvard University." Pinker goes on to opine that until recently people just really did not see anything wrong with genocide "as long as it didn't happen to them."

Out of the "Dark Ages"

Evolution refers to *gradual* growth, a moving forward, a maturing. It is a change for the positive; from simple to more complex. Sometimes such changes can be more sudden and rather dramatic. These changes are termed "revolutions". The "axial age" which I talked about previously was a revolution of morality.. Another important revolution occurred following the Middle Ages in the period now termed the "early modern period". During this period the "Scientific Revolution" began. New developments in physics, biology, chemistry, and mathematics took place, and most importantly the *scientific method* was developed. This is a method for determining reality based on *evidence.*

This led to the "Age of Enlightenment" also known as the "Age of Reason". "Humanism" developed. This is the philosophy that emphasizes rationalism and empiricism with the goal of helping humanity. It stresses kindness and benevolence toward one's fellow human beings. A new school of thought developed which stressed the belief in the inherent worth of all human beings. The belief that the purpose for people was to serve a nation or a monarch was waning. This led to a wave of democratization. A democracy is a government ruled by "the people" in contrast to a monarchy, autocracy or dictatorship (where one individual rules), an oligarchy (rule by a small group of people) or an aristocracy (where rule is by a class of people).

In 1948 a very important document was proclaimed by the United Nations general assembly entitled *The Universal Declaration of Human Rights*. It recognized "the inherent dignity" and "the equal and inalienable rights of all members of the human family" Article 1 of the declaration states "all human beings are born free and equal in dignity and rights.

They are endowed with reason and conscience and should act towards one another in the spirit of brotherhood." Article 3 states "Everyone has the right to life, liberty and security of person." The entire declaration is included in Appendix A of this book.

The Scientific Revolution, The Age of Enlightenment, Humanism, and democracy have all contributed to a decrease in violence and an increase in morality. Pinker (2011) makes a good case that wars are less likely with democracies than other forms of government. Pinker also hypothesizes that reading has contributed to a decrease in violence and an increase in empathy. When reading we get into the mind of others which likely increases our capacity for empathy.

Faustian bargains

I believe that there has been an evolution in empathy, morality, benevolence and love (agape) from the beginnings of our species and even prior to that. Homo sapiens continue to be very selfish and self-centered, however. We often will give up our integrity and convictions to appease self-interests. This theme is reflected in the classic German legend about the character Faust. Faust is a scholar who is unhappy with his life. He wishes for increased knowledge and pleasure, and to accomplish this goal he makes a bargain with a representative of the devil. He gives up his soul in order to have his wishes granted for several years. At the end of this period of time the devil can claim his soul. In some versions of the story Faust is carried off to Hell in the end. In other versions of the story he ends up being saved by God.

This theme has struck such a cord with people that it has been written and re-written over and over again in prose, plays, operas and ballets. Wikipedia has "Works based on Faust" as a topic heading; I suggest the reader look this up on the internet and take notice of the dozens if not hundreds of works of art based on this theme.

It is a common theme in art because it is a common theme in real life. People often give up their principles if it benefits them personally. People will often capitulate to an evil entity (a devil) to save their own skin or that of family members. Think of all the average and generally "good" Catholics and Lutherans who capitulated and appeased the evil devil, Hitler.

A Prayer for Evolution

It is my hope and prayer that humanity continues to evolve, perhaps to what Teilhard de Chardin termed an "Omega Point", a time when all of creation reaches a final point of "divine unification". All of our problems as a species are due to our continuing problems with selfishness, greed and self-centeredness. Wars, poverty, climate change, discrimination, crime, and abuse are the result of self-centeredness and selfishness. All of it is really unnecessary! We don't have to keep thinking in zero-sum terms. I don't have to think that others' gains are my loss. I can realize that I benefit when others benefit. The world, including the United States benefited from the Marshall Plan; although it was financially costly at the time, it has likely greatly paid for itself with unprecedented peace in the world.

World War II in today's dollars cost the United States trillions of dollars. Add to that the cost to the other countries that were Allies (Britain, France, USSR, Australia, Belgium, Brazil, Canada, China, Denmark, Greece, Netherlands, New Zealand, Norway, Poland, South Africa and Yugoslavia) and also the Axis countries (Germany, Italy, Japan, Hungary, Romania, and Bulgaria). How many trillions and trillions of dollars were wasted in waging this war? How many trillions of dollars did it cost to rebuild? How many human lives were lost, and how much human suffering resulted? Who would now say that World War II was a good idea or that it was worthwhile. Who would say that the American Civil War, World War I, the Korean War, or the Vietnam War were a benefit to anybody? Just think what could have been done with all those trillions of dollars to help humanity to evolve rather than causing so much destruction and being a hindrance to human evolution.

Now when I say that war is unnecessary, don't misunderstand me and think that I'm saying that we as a country (or as individuals) should not defend ourselves. I believe we were right to enter WWII, for example, and to stop the aggression of the Axis powers. But in retrospect now, I would guess Germany, Italy and Japan would say that their choices back then were not a good idea. I also am not saying that countries, groups, or individuals should not initiate aggressive actions in certain situations. We need police to go after criminals and dangerous people. We need countries to protect the rights of minorities and to prevent genocides, for example. What I am saying is that it was the self-centeredness of *somebodys* that caused wars to occur.

The philosopher Thomas Hobbes in *The Leviathan* wrote that there were "three principal causes of quarrel": competition, diffidence, and glory:

The first maketh men invade for gain; the second for safety; and the third for reputation. The first use violence, to make themselves masters of other men's persons, wives, children and cattle; the second, to defend them; the third, for trifles, as a word, a smile, a different opinion, and any other sign of undervalue, either direct in their persons or by reflection in their kindred, their friends, their nation, their profession, or their name.

Wars are often started for material gain (such as for land, oil, etc.) or because of the need for dominance, glory or ego. The prophet Isaiah writes about a future kingdom of God in which "the wolf shall live with the lamb, the leopard shall lie down with the kid, the calf and the lion and the fatling together, and a little child shall lead them….for the earth will be full of the knowledge of the Lord." Isaiah believes that humanity and the rest of God's creation can evolve. I do as well, and it will be evolving love which causes this. We need to continue to expand our circles of care. We need to resist our tendencies toward selfishness. Love needs to be extended not only to those who are genetically closest to us or to those of our "tribe", but to all people and indeed to all of life. Jesus even advocated that we love our enemies!

Evolution can be defined as the gradual process of development, particularly from something simple to something more complex. Biological evolution, as written about by Charles Darwin and others, is about the biological changes that occur over an extremely slow and gradual process. These changes are the result of genetic mutations. Genes that are beneficial for the survival of an organism tend to get passed on to future generations, while genes that are detrimental tend to die out. So for example, if a particular insect develops a genetic mutation that causes an unpleasant odor to the birds that feast on them, they have a much better chance for survival, and that genetic mutation will be passed on to offspring. The process is called *natural selection*. Biological evolution is a very important concept for understanding "big history" and has important implications for religious beliefs. Also important to "big history" and evolution is a concept called *emergence*; which will be discussed in the next book of this series.

Evolution is also an important concept for individuals. Everyone knows that babies develop into adults, and that there are common ages for reaching various developmental milestones such as first words, first steps and potty training. But development should not cease once one reaches adulthood. Adults hopefully continue to develop cognitively, emotionally, morally and spiritually. Developmental psychology is a field of study that deals with this topic.

As individuals evolve, so do cultures. The Bible, when studied with consideration of the historical contexts in which the various writings were written, demonstrates how religious beliefs changed and developed. All religions developed. Cultures change and develop- and in the same way that individuals within the culture evolve, i.e. cognitively, emotionally, morally and spiritually. Just look at how western culture has evolved just within the last couple hundred years; slavery is almost universally despised, torture is abhorred, and there is increased concern and rights for women, children, animals, and other groups.

For individuals and cultures to evolve there is a need for education. There is a difference between facts and opinions, and we're in a period of history where truth is under assault. In order to evolve we need to learn how to determine truth. That is the role of science. Science is about both a method for determining facts, and the body of knowledge that accumulates from using the scientific method. This will be the topic for the next book in this series. I believe that both science and religion are important, but they have different purposes. Science gives us information about our universe and about reality, but it does not tell us what to do with the knowledge or address how we should live. This, in my opinion, is what religion should be about.

Churches, which have been struggling to survive as institutions for decades and for many have become irrelevant, can, I believe, once again become relevant. People still have a number of needs that churches can address. But churches too need to evolve. Churches are not going to survive if they continue to be anti-science, anti-intellectual, anti-reason, rigid, legalistic, and judgmental. I can conceive of a church that embraces science and knowledge, and that focuses on helping individuals and society to be more moral, more loving, and less selfish. I can conceive of a church that does not struggle with the concept of evolution but actually makes as its mission to encourage evolution.

Each of the books in this series starts with the word "evolution". That is because right now I can think of no other single word that best describes the meaning of life. It explains what happened to the universe from the Big Bang, how biological life developed, how cultures developed, and how the individual life develops. Evolution is about a change from the simple to the more complex. Evolution is directional, and it is this directionality that I believe is the best argument for the existence of God.

Summary

Continuum of Morality

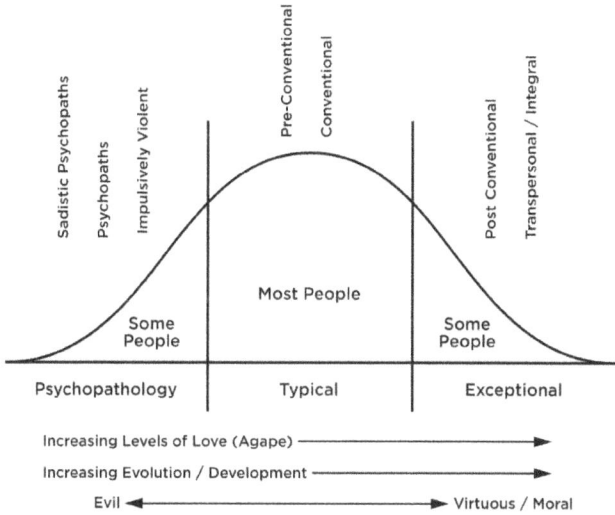

In my opinion there is a continuum of morality based on degrees of selfishness, self-centeredness and greed. People with a psychological disorder known as psychopathy are at the far left end of the continuum. These are people that many would consider as evil. The worst of these are people who are also sadistic. Not only are they completely selfish, but they also *enjoy* the suffering and pain of others. At the far right of the bell curve are those saints who are extraordinarily altruistic and loving. Most of us are somewhere in the middle.

Lawrence Kohlberg is well known for his stages of moral development. Stages one and two are considered *Preconventional Morality*, and at these stages the main motivation is to avoid punishment and to receive rewards. At this stage the child is very self-centered. Around the teenage years most people move into *Conventional Morality*. Right and wrong are defined by authority figures. The focus is on being a "good" person and pleasing society. Some individuals never progress from this stage. Others move into *Post-Conventional Morality*. Here individuals who have developed reasoning abilities are able to abstractly think about morality and realize that societal laws do not always reflect more important moral principals, which for most moral theorists are about love and justice. Some theorize about an even higher level of morality known as *transpersonal* or *integral* in which there is a realization that the entire cosmos is interrelated and that there should be an ever enlarging circle of care to include all of life.

It is my belief that religion should be in the business of promoting love and justice and spiritual development of individuals and of culture. This has rarely been the focus of most churches, however. Most Christian churches have emphasized holding and professing a set of beliefs that religious "authorities" deemed to be "correct" many centuries ago. This, however, was not the message of Jesus. Nor was it the message of the Jewish prophets or of prophets from other religious traditions. In Western culture Christianity is increasingly losing relevance. By returning to a focus on love (agape) and justice, religious communities can be revitalized to become a force for the evolution of life.

Afterword

The case of Donald Trump

This book series, including this particular book, was conceptualized several years ago and long before the Donald Trump candidacy and presidency. I could not help while thinking and writing about morality how the content of this book pertained to what we've been going through as a country. I have written that individuals who are the most immoral are sadistic psychopaths followed by psychopaths in general. I have seen no evidence of Trump being sadistic, but I do maintain that he is a psychopath.

The test considered the "gold standard" for diagnosing psychopathy has been the Hare Psychopathy Checklist-Revised (PCL-R). The items on this test are the following:

1. Glibness/Superficial Charm

2. Grandiose Sense of Self Worth

3. Need for Stimulation/Proneness to Boredom

4. Pathological Lying

5. Conning/Manipulative

6. Lack of Remorse or Guilt

7. Shallow Affect

8. Callous/Lack of Empathy

9. Parasitic Lifestyle

10. Poor Behavioral Controls

11. Promiscuous Sexual Behavior

12. Early Behavioral Problems

13. Lack of Realistic, Long-Term Goals

14. Impulsivity

15. Irresponsibility

16. Failure to Accept Responsibility for Own Actions

17. Many Short-Term Marital Relationships

18. Juvenile Delinquency

19. Revocation of Conditional Release

20. Criminal Versatility

The test is scored using a 3-point scale. An item is scored with two points if it applies to the individual, one point if it maybe applies or applies in some respects, and no points if it does not apply. So an individual can score a maximum of 40 points if they get a score of 2 points on each of the 20 items. Those scoring from 33 to 40 points are in the very high range, and those scoring 25 to 32 points are in the high range. "Most people in the general population would score less than 5 on the PCL-R" (Hare, 2006) By my count I would give Trump a score of 27 points. I believe his privileged background, which includes being put in military school at the age of 13 to keep his energies channeled in a positive direction and his fabulous financial privilege have kept his score from being higher. It is possible that Trump may score additional points in the future if he ends up being convicted for crimes.

The key deficits in a psychopath are lack of empathy and conscience and complete self-centeredness. Hare (1993) has written about some other observations about psychopaths: "Besides being impulsive- doing things on the spur of the moment-psychopaths are highly reactive to perceived insults or slights." (p. 59) "What makes psychopaths different from all others is the remarkable ease with which they lie, the pervasiveness of their deception, and the callousness with which they carry it out." (p. 125)

One might think that a long series of lies would eventually become transparent, leading to unmasking the psychopath, but this is rarely the case. The reason most observers do not see through the lies is that many psychopathic lies serve both to allay the doubts or concerns of the victim and to bolster the psychopathic fiction. Their often theatrical, yet convincing stories and entertaining explanations reinforce an

*environment of trust, acceptance, and genuine delight, lead-
ing most people to accept them exactly as whom they appear
to be- and almost unconsciously excuse any inconsistencies
they might have noted. If challenged or caught in a lie, psychopaths are not embarrassed, They simply change or elab-
orate on the story line to weave together all the misarranged
details into a believable fabric.* (Babiak and Hare, 2006)

I am not the only one who finds serious psychopathology
with Trump. In 2017 *The Dangerous Case of Donald
Trump: 27 Psychiatrists and Mental Health Experts Assess a
President* was published. Most of these mental health pro-
fessionals felt that Trump had a serious personality disorder
and was dangerous. Suggested diagnoses (all very close to
each other in terms of symptomatology) included psychopathy, sociopathy, pathological narcissism and malignant narcissism. This is psychologist John Gartner's 2017 summa-
tion: *"Trump is a profoundly evil man exhibiting malignant
narcissism. His worsening hypomania is making him
increasingly more irrational, grandiose, paranoid, aggressive, irritable, and impulsive. Trump is bad, mad, and getting worse. He evinces the most destructive and dangerous
collection of psychiatric symptoms possible for a leader.
The worst-case scenario is now our reality."* (Lee et al,
2017)

Elizabeth Mika M.A. discussed tyrants in her chapter of this
book. *"Tyrants are dictators gone bad...All tyrants share
several essential features: they are predominantly men with
a specific character defect, narcissistic psychopathy (a.k.a.
malignant narcissism). This defect manifests in a severely
impaired or absent conscience and an insatiable drive for
power and adulation that masks the conscience deficits. It*

forms the core of attraction between him and his followers, the essence of what is seen as his 'charisma'."

Mika says tyrannies are "three-legged beasts". There are three necessary components to a tyranny; the charismatic tyrant, the supporters, and a society that is ripe for the rise of autocracy. Economic inequality makes for fertile ground for the rise of an autocrat. *"Narcissistic psychopaths turned tyrants possess the right combination of manipulativeness, self-control, and intelligence to convince others to support them long enough to put their grandiose ideas to work on a large scale. They also appear to possess skills that are seen as charisma, the most frequent of which is the ability to deliver public speeches that inspire others to follow them. More often than not, however, this 'charisma' is simply their ability to tell others what they want to hear (i.e., to lie), to make them go along with whatever scheme they've concocted for the moment. Their glibness is something that easily fools normal people, who do not understand the kind of pathology that results from a missing conscience."*

How could such a characterologically defective individual be elected president of the United States? How could we elect a a man who actually advocates violence between members of the American populace? The following cartoon created by illustrator Jesse Duquette and fact checked by Snopes gives some examples.

How could people who stress the importance of "family values" endorse a man who has been accused by at least 19 women of sexual assault and/or harassment? Some have been paid off for their silence. He bragged about his ability (on tape) to sexually assault women, i.e. that he's able to grab them by their private parts. How can people who are for "family values" be alright with marital infidelity and the absence of active fathering while offspring are in their childhood (when have you ever heard of Trump actively involved in his son Baron's life, such as taking him golfing, an activity he does all the time)? How can people who advocate family values be okay with thousands of children being taken forcefully away from their parents at the southern border? How can people endorse a U.S. president who cannot completely denounce Nazism or the Klu Klux Klan?

How can Republicans ignore some of the most basic core ideologies of their party, i.e. the importance of the rule of law and opposition to communism, especially Russia? Remember that Ronald Reagan characterized the Soviet Union as the "evil empire." Putin, the ex-KGB agent who kills journalists, is given nothing but praise by Trump. How can some leaders of our country ignore insults to other democratic nations while Trump heaps praise on autocratic strongmen such as Kim Jong-un of North Korea, Recep Tayyip Erdoğan of Turkey, and Rodrigo Duterte of the Philippines? How can leaders of this country tolerate the present indifference to human rights? The United States' past leadership on the topic of human rights was one of our greatest virtues. Ronald Reagan said, "America is a shining city upon a hill whose beacon light guides freedom-loving people everywhere". Now we have a president who denigrates democracies, praises tyrants and states that white supremacists and Nazis are "good people too".

The Washington Post has been tracking the number of "false or misleading claims" of the president, and at January 21, 2019 they tabulated 8,158 such false claims (6,000 of the claims occurred in his second year of office). That averages out to be almost 16.5 false claims per day in that second year. Politicians have always been known to "spin" and prevaricate, but prior to this presidency I do not recall a politician, much less a president, being characterized regularly and routinely by many as a "liar". How can these chronic lies be tolerated and ignored by so many people?

What if we were to train our children to be like our current president of the United States? What if we taught our 4 and 5- year old children in preparation for kindergarten to never admit you are wrong. When somebody criticizes you do not listen to them or consider their perspective, but rather go after them and criticize them for something ten times harder. If you find somebody weak or vulnerable, go after them. The best way to get ahead in kindergarten is to develop enemies. If you make fun of others, you will raise yourself up. Bullying is fine; do whatever it takes to be number one. Do not follow the golden rule. Don't do for others what you wish for yourself; rather do to them whatever it is that gets you ahead. There are winners and losers. Make sure you do everything you can by any means to get ahead and to win. It is okay to lie and cheat- as long as you win and don't get caught.

At this point in time I think few parents would teach these values to their children. Yet many of us seem to think, unbelievably, that this is acceptable behavior for the president of the United States! We have long made rationalizations for the lack of honesty and integrity of politicians. We say, "that's just politics". It is time to no longer tolerate this. We should expect *more*, not less, from our leaders. In democracies, unlike monarchies and aristocracies, we should expect our leaders to *serve* the people of the country, rather than the old inverse paradigm of the populace's purpose being to serve its leaders.

The "me too movement" is about a change in paradigm. We are moving away from the excuse of "boys will be boys". We need a change of paradigm in American politics as well; no longer should we find acceptable the phrase "that's just politics". We should expect honesty and integrity in our leaders. For leaders to work against a country's interests and in service of their own personal interests is basically treason, if not in the legal sense.

Why do average, normal people go along with evil? The Faust myth gives us much of the answer. We will make a deal with the devil if we believe it benefits us sufficiently. We'll make allowances for immorality if we get a tax cut, or if we're a miner or factory worker and we're promised that our industry will be revitalized. We'll go along with a psychopath if they tell us what we want to hear and if they tap into anger and hatred that we already have. People look for scapegoats for hateful feelings. For a long time in recent memory homosexuals were a major source of fear and hatred. Now since so many have "come out of the closet" and we find that many are our family members and friends (and so in our tribe), new targets of hatred have lately predominated. Racism seems also to have come back out of the closet and made a resurgence. Hispanics and Muslims have become a prime target of fear and hate. Politicians also become willing sycophants and enablers to stay in power themselves and not be "primaried".

What is most concerning to me and many of my friends is not the evil of Donald Trump and others like him, but rather how so many average people can disregard such immorality in the service of perceived self-interests. The other thing that greatly bothers me and many of my friends is the disregard for truth. Reality does exist. Truth is not relative. This is a major topic for the next book in this series. We need to rediscover the ideals of Superman, i.e. the need for truth, justice, and the American way (which to me is democracy).

Study Questions

Introduction

What is morality?

What does it mean to be morally "good" or morally "bad"?

How important is the "golden rule" to your religious beliefs?

Are there religious beliefs or ideas that are more important than the golden rule?

Are there any ways that you think the golden rule could be improved upon?

What are your beliefs about special revelation?

What is the difference between sin and evil?

Can morality exist without God?

Would people be moral without the "carrot and stick" of a belief in heaven and hell?

Are there moral absolutes, or is morality relative?

What are your thoughts about determinism (the doctrine that all events, including human action, are ultimately determined by causes external to the will) and the doctrine of predestination?

Chapter One

Do you believe that some animals other than humans have a sense of morality? Can animals be immoral?

Theodicy concerns itself with the question of why evil exists in the presence of an omnipotent and loving God. How would you explain this?

Why do natural evils exist? For example, why do natural disasters exist that kill thousands of people?

If Satan is the tempter that causes people to do evil, why do some succumb and others do not?

Is Christianity a monotheistic religion? Explain why you answer yes or no to this.

Do you agree with the author's statement that "much of religion even to this day seems to be only to serve self-interests"?

Do you agree with Joseph Fletcher that love is the only thing that is intrinsically good?

Do you agree with the author that behaviors done out of love make the behaviors moral?

Can there be moral absolutes without a belief in God?

What makes behaviors or thoughts "immoral"?

Chapter Two

What is evil? What causes it?

Do you agree that evil is psychopathology? What makes people evil?

What is your reaction to the statement that "love leads to evolution"?

What are your thoughts about the story of the wave as a metaphor?

What makes a behavior evil? Are some actions inherently evil? Do the consequences of an action contribute to the formula of what makes an action evil? Are the intentions of the actor an important factor in determining if something is evil?

It is currently somewhat of a taboo in our society for comparing any evil person to Adolf Hitler. Do you agree with this taboo?

Chapter Three

What are your reactions to the information about sex and gender?

What are your reactions to the information on Kohlberg's stages of moral development? Do you believe there are stages of moral development?

Why is it that the Supreme Court, rather than legislatures, has been the entity that has been responsible for giving more rights to various groups of people?

What is the relationship between morality and justice?

Do you agree with Haidt's view that morality is a cultural construction and people have various moral "tastes"?

Is "authority" a foundational concept for you when considering morality?

Is "loyalty" a foundational concept for you when considering morality?

Is "sanctity and purity" a foundational concept for you when considering morality?

Is it immoral to burn an American flag? Is the flag "sacred"?

What things would you consider as being "sacred" and why?

Is intuition useful for making moral judgments?

What do you think predominates for people in making moral judgments- emotion or reason?

Do you agree with the author that changes in prejudice occur due to changes in emotional reaction and not due to reason?

Do you believe that good and evil are on a continuum?

Do you agree that evil is primarily about selfishness?

What are your thoughts about Vander Maas's "Continuum of Morality"?

Chapter Four

What do you believe was the primary teaching of Jesus?

What do you believe is the primary teaching of the Christian church today?

Do you believe there has been a "corruption of Christianity"?

Do you concur with Pinker that humanity has become less violent and more moral?

Do you agree with the author that all of our major problems as a species are primarily due to self-centeredness and self-ishness?

Is it legitimate to you to judge our leaders' moral character? What is the criteria we should use to judge someone's moral character?

How important is it for leaders to be moral? What would be good reasons for you to vote for an individual despite serious deficits in moral character?

What is your reaction to the author's statement that "evolution" is the best word to characterize the meaning of life? Do you have a better word?

Do you believe that evolution is directional? Does evolution have a purpose?

Appendix A
The Universal Declaration of Human Rights
Resolution of the UN General Assembly
1948

Preamble
Whereas recognition of the inherent dignity and of the equal and
inalienable rights of all members of the human family is the foundation of freedom, justice and peace in the world,

Whereas disregard and contempt for human rights have resulted in
barbarous acts which have outraged the conscience of mankind,
and the advent of a world in which human beings shall enjoy freedom of speech and belief and freedom from fear and want has been
proclaimed as the highest aspiration of the common people,

Whereas it is essential, if man is not to be compelled to have
recourse, as a last resort, to rebellion against tyranny and oppression, that human rights should be protected by the rule of law,

Whereas it is essential to promote the development of friendly relations between nations, Whereas the peoples of the United Nations
have in the Charter reaffirmed their faith in fundamental human
rights, in the dignity and worth of the human person and in the
equal rights of men and women and have determined to promote
social progress and better standards of life in larger freedom,

Whereas Member States have pledged themselves to achieve, in cooperation with the United Nations, the promotion of universal respect for and observance of human rights and fundamental freedoms,
Whereas a common understanding of these rights and freedoms is of the greatest importance for the full realization of this pledge,
Now, therefore,

The General Assembly, Proclaims this Universal Declaration of Human Rights as a common standard of achievement for all peoples and all nations, to the end that every individual and every organ of society, keeping this Declaration constantly in mind, shall strive by teaching and education to promote respect for these rights and freedoms and by progressive measures, national and international, to secure their universal and effective recognition and observance, both among the peoples of Member States themselves and among the peoples of territories under their jurisdiction.

Article I
All human beings are born free and equal in dignity and rights. They are endowed with reason and conscience and should act towards one another in a spirit of brotherhood.

Article 2
Everyone is entitled to all the rights and freedoms set forth in this Declaration, without distinction of any kind, such as race, colour, sex, language, religion, political or other opinion, national or social origin, property, birth or other status. Furthermore, no distinction shall be made on the basis of the political, jurisdictional or international status of the country or territory to which a person belongs, whether it be independent, trust, non-self-governing or under any other limitation of sovereignty.

Article 3
Everyone has the right to life, liberty and security of person.

Article 4
No one shall be held in slavery or servitude; slavery and the slave trade shall be prohibited in all their forms.

Article 5
No one shall be subjected to torture or to cruel, inhuman or degrading treatment or punishment.

Article 6
Everyone has the right to recognition everywhere as a person before the law.

Article 7
All are equal before the law and are entitled without any discrimination to equal protection of the law. All are entitled to equal protection against any discrimination in violation of this Declaration and against any incitement to such discrimination.

Article 8
Everyone has the right to an effective remedy by the competent national tribunals for acts violating the fundamental rights granted him by the constitution or by law.

Article 9
No one shall be subjected to arbitrary arrest, detention or exile.

Article 10
Everyone is entitled in full equality to a fair and public hearing by an independent and impartial tribunal, in the determination of his rights and obligations and of any criminal charge against him.

Article 11
1. Everyone charged with a penal offence has the right to be presumed innocent until proved guilty according to law in a public trial at which he has had all the guarantees necessary for his defence.

2. No one shall be held guilty of any penal offence on account of any act or omission which did not constitute a penal offence, under national or international law, at the time when it was committed. Nor shall a heavier penalty be imposed than the one that was applicable at the time the penal offence was committed.

Article 12
No one shall be subjected to arbitrary interference with his privacy, family, home or correspondence, nor to attacks upon his honour and reputation. Everyone has the right to the protection of the law against such interference or attacks.

Article 13
1. Everyone has the right to freedom of movement and residence within the borders of each State.
2. Everyone has the right to leave any country, including his own, and to return to his country.

Article 14
1. Everyone has the right to seek and to enjoy in other countries asylum from persecution.
2. This right may not be invoked in the case of prosecutions genuinely arising from non-political crimes or from acts contrary to the purposes and principles of the United Nations.

Article 15
1. Everyone has the right to a nationality.
2. No one shall be arbitrarily deprived of his nationality nor denied the right to change his nationality.

Article 16
1. Men and women of full age, without any limitation due to race, nationality or religion, have the right to marry and to found a family. They are entitled to equal rights as to marriage, during marriage and at its dissolution.
2. Marriage shall be entered into only with the free and full consent of the intending spouses.

3. The family is the natural and fundamental group unit of society and is entitled to protection by society and the State.

Article 17
1. Everyone has the right to own property alone as well as in association with others.
2. No one shall be arbitrarily deprived of his property.

Article 18 Everyone has the right to freedom of thought, conscience and religion; this right includes freedom to change his religion or belief, and freedom, either alone or in community with others and in public or private, to manifest his religion or belief in teaching, practice, worship and observance.

Article 19 Everyone has the right to freedom of opinion and expression; this right includes freedom to hold opinions without interference and to seek, receive and impart information and ideas through any media and regardless of frontiers.

Article 20
1. Everyone has the right to freedom of peaceful assembly and association.
2. No one may be compelled to belong to an association.

Article 21
1. Everyone has the right to take part in the government of his country, directly or through freely chosen representatives.
2. Everyone has the right to equal access to public service in his country.
3. The will of the people shall be the basis of the authority of government; this will shall be expressed in periodic and genuine elections which shall be by universal and equal suffrage and shall be held by secret vote or by equivalent free voting procedures.

Article 22
Everyone, as a member of society, has the right to social security and is entitled to realization, through national effort and interna-

tional co-operation and in accordance with the organization and resources of each State, of the economic, social and cultural rights indispensable for his dignity and the free development of his personality.

Article 23

1. Everyone has the right to work, to free choice of employment, to just and favourable conditions of work and to protection against unemployment.

2. Everyone, without any discrimination, has the right to equal pay for equal work.

3. Everyone who works has the right to just and favourable remuneration ensuring for himself and his family an existence worthy of human dignity, and supplemented, if necessary, by other means of social protection.

4. Everyone has the right to form and to join trade unions for the protection of his interests.

Article 24

Everyone has the right to rest and leisure, including reasonable limitation of working hours and periodic holidays with pay.

Article 25

1. Everyone has the right to a standard of living adequate for the health and well-being of himself and of his family, including food, clothing, housing and medical care and necessary social services, and the right to security in the event of unemployment, sickness, disability, widowhood, old age or other lack of livelihood in circumstances beyond his control.

2. Motherhood and childhood are entitled to special care and assistance. All children, whether born in or out of wedlock, shall enjoy the same social protection.

Article 26

1. Everyone has the right to education. Education shall be free, at least in the elementary and fundamental stages. Elementary education shall be compulsory. Technical and professional education

shall be made generally available and higher education shall be equally accessible to all on the basis of merit.

2. Education shall be directed to the full development of the human personality and to the strengthening of respect for human rights and fundamental freedoms. It shall promote understanding, tolerance and friendship among all nations, racial or religious groups, and shall further the activities of the United Nations for the maintenance of peace.

3. Parents have a prior right to choose the kind of education that shall be given to their children.

Article 27

1. Everyone has the right freely to participate in the cultural life of the community, to enjoy the arts and to share in scientific advancement and its benefits.

2. Everyone has the right to the protection of the moral and material interests resulting from any scientific, literary or artistic production of which he is the author.

Article 28

Everyone is entitled to a social and international order in which the rights and freedoms set forth in this Declaration can be fully realized.

Article 29

1. Everyone has duties to the community in which alone the free and full development of his personality is possible.

2. In the exercise of his rights and freedoms, everyone shall be subject only to such limitations as are determined by law solely for the purpose of securing due recognition and respect for the rights and freedoms of others and of meeting the just requirements of morality, public order and the general welfare in a democratic society.

3. These rights and freedoms may in no case be exercised contrary to the purposes and principles of the United Nations.

Article 30 Nothing in this Declaration may be interpreted as implying for any State, group or person any right to engage in any activity or to perform any act aimed at the destruction of any of the rights and freedoms set forth herein.

Bibliography

Introduction

Anda, Robert F., Felitti, Vincent J., Bremner, J. Douglas, Walker, John D., Whitfield, Charles, Perry, Bruce D., Dube, Shanta R. and Giles, Wayne H. The enduring effects of abuse and related adverse experiences in childhood: a convergence of evidence from neurobiology and epidemiology. European Archives of Psychiatry and Clinical Neuroscience 2006 Apr; 256(3): 174-186.

Jensen, Dan (2017). *A False Kind of Christianity: A Conservative Evangelical Refutation of Progressive Christianity*. Grand Rapids; Westbow Press.

Rand, Ayn (1964). *The Virtue of Selfishness*. New York: Signet.

Chapter One

Alighieri, Dante (1995). *The Divine Comedy.* New York: Alfred A. Knopf.

Aslan, Reza (2013). *Zealot: The Life and Times of Jesus of Nazareth.* New York: Random House.

Bekoff, M. and Pierce, J. (2009). *Wild Justice: The Moral Lives of Animals.* Chicago: The University of Chicago Press.

Big Book, Third Edition (1976). New York: Alcoholics Anonymous World Services, Inc.

Boehm, C. (2012). *Moral Origins: The Evolution of Virtue, Altruism, and Shame.* New York: Basic Books.

Casey, John (2009). *After Lives: A Guide to Heaven, Hell and Purgatory.* New York: Oxford University Press.

Charles, R.H., translator. (2011). *The Book of Jubilees.* Merchant Books.

Darwin, C. (1982 [1871]). *The Descent of Man, and Selection in Relation to Sex.* Princeton: Princeton University Press.

De Waal, F. (1996). *Good Natured: The Origins of Right and Wrong in Humans and Other Animals.* Cambridge, MA: Harvard University Press.

De Waal, F. (2006). *Primates and Philosophers*. Princeton, NJ: Princeton University Press.

De Waal, F. (2013). *The Bonobo and the Atheist.* New York: W.W. Norton & Co.

Fletcher, Joseph (1966). *Situation Ethics*. Philadelphia, PA: Westminster Press.

Forsyth, Neil (1987). *The Old Enemy: Satan and the Combat Myth*. Princeton, NJ: Princeton University Press.

Fowler, James W. (1995). *Stages of Faith: The Psychology of Human Development and the Quest for Meaning*. New York: Harper One.

Hopfe, Lewis and Woodward, Mark (2009). *Religions of the World, 11th Ed.* New Jersey: Pearson Education.

King, Barbara (2007). *Evolving God: A Provocative View on the Origins of Religion*. Chicago: University of Chicago Press.

Lumpkin, Joseph B. (2009). *The First and Second Books of Adam and Eve: The Conflict with Satan*. Blountsville, AL: Fifth Estate.

Lumpkin, Joseph B. (2011). *The Books of Enoch: The Angels, The Watchers and The Nephilim, 2nd Ed.* Blountsville, AL: Fifth Estate.

Milton, John (1674). *Paradise Lost.* Oxford: Oxford University Press.

Pagels, Elaine (1995). *The Origin of Satan.* New York: Random House.

Peck, M. Scott (1978). *The Road Less Traveled.* New York: Touchstone.

Prüfer, Kay, et al. (2012). The bonobo genome compared with the chimpanzee and human genomes. Nature doi:10.1038/nature11128

Russell, Jeffrey Burton (1977). *The Devil: Perceptions of Evil from Antiquity to Primitive Christianity.* Ithica: Cornell University Press.

Russell, Jeffrey Burton (1981). *Satan: The Early Christian Tradition.* Ithica: Cornell University Press.

Russell, Jeffrey Burton (1984). *Lucifer: The Devil in the Middle Ages.* Ithica: Cornell University Press.

Sapolsky, Robert M. (2017). *Behave: The Biology of Humans at Our Best and Worst.* New York: Penguin Press.

Stark, Rodney (2008). *What Americans Really Believe.* Waco, TX: Baylor University Press.

Trivers, R.L. (1971). The evolution of reciprocal altruism. *Quarterly Review of Biology* 46:35-57.

Vander Maas, Craig (2017). *Evolution and Syncretism of Religion.* Grand Rapids: Integral Growth Publishing.

Van Der Toorn, K., Becking, B. & Van Der Horst, P. (1999). *Dictionary of Deities and Demons in the Bible, 2nd ed.* Grand Rapids: Wm. Eerdmans Publishing.

Wrangham, R. & Peterson, D. (1996). *Demonic Males: Apes and the Origins of Human Violence.* London:Bloomsbury Publishing.

Wray, T.J. & Mobley, Gregory (2005). *The Birth of Satan: Tracing the Devil's Biblical Roots.* New York: Palgrave Macmillan.

Zahn-Waxler, C., B. Hollenbeck, and M. Radke-Yarrow. 1984. The origins of empathy and altruism. In *Advances in Animal Welfare Science*, ed. M.W. Fox and L.D. Mickley, pp. 21-39. Washington, DC: Humane Society of the United States.

Chapter Two

Albom, Mitch (1997). *Tuesdays with Morrie*. New York: Doubleday.

Amen, D., Hanks, C., Prunella, J. & Green, A. (2007). An analysis of regional cerebral blood flow in impulsive murderers using single photon emission computed tomography. Journal of Neuropsychiatry and Clinical Neurosciences 19, 304-9.

Anda, R., Felitti, V., Bremner, J.D., Walker, J., Whitfield, C., Perry, B., Dube, S., & Giles, W. (2006). The enduring effects of abuse and related adverse experiences in childhood. Eur Arch Psychiatry Clinical Neuroscience. April; 256(3): 174-186.

American Psychiatric Association (2013). *Diagnostic and Statistical Manual of Mental Disorders, Fifth Edition*. Arlington, VA: American Psychiatric Association.

Andersen, Kurt (2017). *Fantasyland: How America Went Haywire*. New York: Random House.

Babiak, Paul and Hare, Robert (2006). *Snakes in Suits: When Psychopaths Go to Work*. New York: Harper Collins.

Baron-Cohen, Simon (2011). *The Science of Evil: On Empathy and the Origins of Cruelty*. New York: Basic Books.

Blair, R.J.R. (2008). The amygdala and ventromedial pre-frontal cortex: functional contributions and dysfunction in psychopathy. Phil. Trans. R. Soc. B (2008) 363, 2557-2565.

Bouchard, T.J. & McGue, M. (2003). Genetic and environ-mental influences on human psychological differences. Journal of Neurobiology 54, 4-45.

Bowlby, J. (1946). *Forty-four Juvenile Thieves: Their Characters and Home-life*. London: Tindall and Cox.

Cherkasky, S. & Hollander, E. (2005). Neuropsychiatric Aspects of Impulsivity and Aggression. In *Textbook of Neuropsychiatry*. Washington, DC: American Psychiatric Press.

Cleckley, Hervey (1982). *The Mask of Sanity*. New York: Plume.

Damasio, Antonio (1994). *Descartes' Error: Emotion, Reason, and the Human Brain*. New York: Grosset/Putnam Books.

Dawkins, Richard (1989). *The Selfish Gene*. Oxford, United Kingdom: Oxford University Press.

Fletcher, Joseph (1966). *Situation Ethics: The New Morality*. Philadelphia, PA: Westminster Press.

Fromm, Erich (1964). *The Heart of Man*. Riverdale NY: American Mental Health Foundation.

Fromm, Erich (1973). *The Anatomy of Human Destructiveness*. New York: Piador.

Hare, Robert (1993). *Without Conscience: The Disturbing World of the Psychopaths Among Us*. New York: Guilford Press.

Hare, Robert (2003). Hare Psychopathology Checklist-Revised (PCL-R): 2nd Edition Technical Manual. North Tonawanda, NY: MHS.

Kernberg, Otto (1992). *Aggression in Personality Disorders and Perversions*. New Haven: Yale University Press.

Kiehl, K. (2006). A cognitive neuroscience perspective on psychopathy: Evidence for paralimbic system dysfunction. Psychiatry Research 142, 107-28.

Koenigs, M. (2012). The role of prefrontal cortex in psychopathy. Reviews in the Neurosciences 2012; 23(3): 253-262.

Larsson, H., Andershed, H., & Lichtenstein, P. (2006). A genetic factor explains most of the variation in the psychopathic personality. Journal of Abnormal Psychology, 115(2), 221-230.

Látalová, K. (2009). Bipolar disorder and aggression. The International Journal of Clinical Practice 13 May 2009.

Levack, Brian (2013). *The Devil Within: Possession & Exorcism in the Christian West*. New Haven: Yale University Press.

Malik, Kenan (2014). *The Quest for a Moral Compass: A Global History of Ethics*. Brooklyn, NY: Melville House Publishing.

Mendez, J.F., Chen A.K., Shapira, J.S. & Miller B.L. (2005). Acquired sociopathy and frontotemporal dementia. Dementia and Geriatric Cognitive Disorders 2005; 20:99-104.

Mendez, M.F. & Shapira, J.S. (2013). Hypersexual behavior in frontotemporal dementia: a comparison with early-onset alzheimer's disease. Archives of Sexual Behavior 2013 April: 42(3): 501-509.

Miczek, K. & Fish, E. (2006). Monoamines, GABA, Glutamate, and Aggression. In *Biology of Aggression*. New York: Oxford University Press.

Muller, J., Sommer, M., Wagner, V., Lange, K., Taschler, H., et al. (2003). Abnormalities in emotion processing within cortical and subcortical regions in criminal psychopaths: Evidence from a functional magnetic resonance imaging study using pictures with emotional content. Biological Psychiatry 54, 152-62.

Nelson, Randy (2006). *Biology of Aggression*. New York: Oxford University Press.

Pinker, Steven (2011). *The Better Angels of Our Nature: Why Violence Has Declined*. New York: Penguin Books.

Price, T., Goetz, K. & Lovell, M. (2005). Neuropsychiatric Aspects of Brain Tumors. In *Textbook of Neuropsychiatry*. Washington, DC: American Psychiatric Press.

Raine, Adrian (2014). *The Anatomy of Violence: The Biological Roots of Crime*. New York: Vintage Books.

Sapolsky, Robert (2017). *Behave: The Biology of Humans at Our Best and Worst*. New York: Penguin Press.

Scarpa, A. and Raine, A. (2006). The psychophysiology of human antisocial behavior. In *Biology of Aggression*. New York: Oxford University Press.

Shamay-Tsoory, S., Aharon-Peretz, J. & Perry, D. (2009). Two systems for empathy: a double dissociation between emotional and cognitive empathy in inferior frontal gyrus versus ventromedial prefrontal lesions. Brain: A Journal of Neurology 132; 617-627.

Shermer, Michael (2004). *The Science of Good and Evil*. New York: Holt Paperbacks.

Soderstrom, H., Tullberg, M., Wikkelso, C., Ekholm, S. & Forsman, A. (2000). Reduced regional cerebral blood flow in non-psychotic violent offenders. Psychiatry Research: Neuroimaging 98, 29-41.

Stone, M. (2009). *The Anatomy of Evil*. Amherst, New York: Prometheus.

Waldrop, M. F., Bell, R.Q., McLaughlin, B. & Halverson, C.F. (1978). Newborn minor physical anomalies predict attention span, peer aggression, and impulsivity at age 3. Science 199, 563-65.

White, K. & Cummings, J. (2005). Neuropsychiatric Aspects of Alzheimer's Disease and Other Dementing Illnesses. In *Textbook of Neuropsychiatry*. Washington, DC: American Psychiatric Press.

Wrangham, Richard & Peterson, Dale. (1996). *Demonic Males: Apes and the Origins of Human Violence*. London: Bloomsbury Publishing.

Chapter Three

Damasio, Antonio (1994). *Descartes' Error: Emotion, Reason, and the Human Brain*. New York: Grosset/Putnam Books.

Fletcher, Joseph (1966). *Situation Ethics*. Philadelphia, PA: Westminster Press.

Fowler, James W. (1981). *Stages of Faith: The Psychology of Human Development and the Quest for Meaning*. New York: HarperCollins.

Freud (1920). *Beyond the Pleasure Principle.*

Freud (1923). *The Ego and the Id.*

Gibbs, John (2014). *Moral Development and Realty: Beyond the Theories of Kohlberg, Hoffman, and Haidt*. New York: Oxford University Press.

Gilligan, Carol (1982). *In a Different Voice: Psychological Theory and Women's Development*. Cambridge: Harvard University Press.

Haidt, Jonathan (2012). *The Righteous Mind: Why Good People Are Divided by Politics and Religion*. New York: Vintage Books.

Hatemi, P., Gillespie, N., Eaves, L., Maher, B., Webb, B., Heath, A., Medland, S., Smyth, D., Beeby, H., Gordon, S., Montgomery, G., Zhu, G., Byrne, E., & Martin, N. (2011). A genome-wide analysis of liberal and conservative political attitudes. The Journal of Politics Vol. 73, No. 1.

Kohlberg, Lawrence (1971). Stages of moral development as a basis for moral education. In Beck, C.M., Crittenden, B.S. & Sullivan, E.V. (Eds), *Moral Education: Interdisciplinary Approaches*. New York: Newman Press.

Kohlberg, L. & Power, C. (1981). Moral development, religious thinking, and the question of a seventh stage. In Kohlberg, Lawrence, *Essays on Moral Development Vol. 1: Philosophy of Moral Development*. San Francisco, CA: Harper & Row.

Kohlberg, L. & Ryncarz, R.A. (1990). Beyond justice reasoning: moral development and consideration of a seventh stage. In C.N. Alexander & E.J. Langer (Eds.), *Higher stages of human development: perspectives on adult growth*. New York: Oxford University Press.

LeVay, S., Baldwin, J., and Baldwin, J. (2015). *Discovering Human Sexuality, 3rd Edition*. Sunderland, Massachusetts: Sinauer Associates, Inc.

Maslow, A. (1971). *The Farther Reaches of Human Nature*. New York: Viking Pess.

Maslow, A. (2014). *Toward a Psychology of Being*. Floyd VA: Sublime Books.

Navarrete, C. & Fessler, D. (2006). Disease avoidance and ethnocentrism: the effects of disease vulnerability and disgust sensitivity on intergroup attitudes. Evolution and Human Behavior 27 (4) 270-282.

Pinker, Steven (2011). *The Better Angels of Our Nature: Why Violence Has Declined.* New York: Penguin.

Reich, Robert (2013). *Aftershock: The Next Economy and America's Future.* New York: Vintage Books.

Singer, Peter (1981). *The Expanding Circle: Ethics, Evolution, and Moral Progress.* Princeton, New Jersey: Princeton University Press.

Sapolsky, Robert (2017). *Behave: The Biology of Humans at Our Best and Worst.* New York: Penguin Press.

Chapter Four

Borg, Marcus (1994). *Meeting Jesus Again for the First Time: The Historical Jesus & the Heart of Contemporary Faith*. New York: Harper Collins.

Chomsky, Noam (2017). *Requiem for the American Dream: The 10 Principles of Concentration of Wealth and Power.* New York: Seven Stories Press.

Demause, Lloyd (1982). *Foundations of Psychohistory*. New York: Creative Roots Publishing.

Pinker, Steven (2011). *The Better Angels of Our Nature: Why Violence Has Declined.* New York: Penguin.

Reich, Robert (2011). *Aftershock: The Next Economy and America's Future*. New York: Vintage Books.

Reich, Robert (2015). *Saving Capitalism: For the Many, Not the Few.* New York: Vintage Books.

Rozycka-Tran, J., Boski, P., & Wojciszke, B. (2015). Belief in a zero-sum game as a social axiom: a 37-nation study. Journal of Cross-Cultural Psychology 46 (4): 525-548.

Scotton, Bruce (1996). Introduction and definition of transpersonal psychiatry. In Scotton, B., Chinen, A. and Battista, J. (Eds) *Textbook of Transpersonal Psychiatry and Psychology*. New York: Basic Books.

Vander Maas, Craig (2017). *Evolution and Syncretism of Religion: An Integral and Evolutionary World View*. Grand Rapids, MI: Integral Growth Publishing.

Walsh, Roger & Vaughan, Frances (1993). On transpersonal definitions. Journal of Transpersonal Psychology, Vol. 25, No. 2.

Wrangham, R. & Peterson, Dale (1997). *Demonic Males: Apes and the Origins of Human Violence*. London: Bloomsbury.

Wright, Robert (2000). *NonZero: The Logic of Human Destiny*. New York: Pantheon Books.

Afterward

Babiak, Paul and Hare, Robert (2006). *Snakes in Suits: When Psychopaths Go to Work*. New York: Harper Collins.

Hare, Robert (1993). *Without Conscience: The Disturbing World of the Psychopaths Among Us*. New York: Guilford Press.

Lee, Bandy (Ed) (2017). *The Dangerous Case of Donald Trump: 27 Psychiatrists and Mental Health Experts Assess a President*. New York: St. Martin's Press.

Mika, Elizabeth (2017). Who Goes Trump? Tyranny as a Triumph of Narcissism. In Lee, B. (Ed) *The Dangerous Case of Donald Trump: 27 Psychiatrists and Mental Health Experts Assess a President.* New York: St. Martin's Press.

Index

www.ingramcontent.com/pod-product-compliance
Lightning Source LLC
LaVergne TN
LVHW051502080426
835509LV00017B/1878